PRAISE FOR AMERICA NEEDS TALENT AND JAMIE MERISOTIS

"America Needs Talent offers a sharp, timely blueprint for unleashing the potential of millions of Americans. This is the path toward not just individual and familial success but also urban and national prosperity."

—*Bruce Katz, Vice President and Founding Director of the Brookings Metropolitan Policy Program*

"Jamie Merisotis moves us beyond old debates and one-dimensional solutions to respond to one of our country's greatest challenges. *America Needs Talent* makes it clear that if we're willing to harness the innovation born of cross-sector collaboration and embrace new ways to accomplish our goals, we can nurture the talent we need to make the story of 21st-century America one of truly inclusive prosperity."

—*Melody Barnes, Former Assistant to President Barack Obama and Director of the Domestic Policy Council*

"From accountability in higher education to a more strategic approach to immigration, Jamie Merisotis makes a strong case for a deliberate, national talent policy that can develop and deploy the most talented citizenry in the world."

—*Mitch Daniels, President of Purdue University and former Indiana Governor*

"This book is a must-read for anyone who is worried about America's role in the 21st century and looking for solutions."

—*John R. McKernan, Jr., Senior Adviser, US Chamber of Commerce and former Governor of Maine*

"Merisotis is dead right: If we don't fix higher education and build new kinds of public-private partnerships, with employers of all types, America will lose the global war for good jobs."

—*Jim Clifton, Chairman and CEO, Gallup*

"What a refreshing and important antidote to the conventional wisdom about America's future. Just when so many thinkers are focused on robots and the threat that automation will close off possibilities for Americans, Jamie Merisotis understands that the opposite is true—that the future will put even more of a premium on human beings and their talent. He's right to be hopeful, but also right to goad us: we won't realize our great potential unless we start to do things differently—focusing on talent and cultivating it with all the tools at our disposal."

—*Tamar Jacoby, President, Opportunity America*

"In *America Needs Talent*, Jamie Merisotis identifies critical solutions to the biggest problems our cities face today, from immigration to spurring innovation. Merisotis details these solutions with a constant refrain that competitiveness, compassion, and equity must be priorities. *America Needs Talent* offers a blueprint for a Second American Century—one that I believe, as Mayor of Louisville, will make our communities more vibrant, and our nation more prosperous."

—*Greg Fischer, Mayor of Louisville*

"In his fresh-voiced and accessible style, Merisotis makes the compelling argument for why and how higher education must be turned on its head so that we can build a strong new American Century in which people from all walks of life can participate and benefit."

—*Nancy Zimpher, Chancellor, State University of New York*

AMERICA NEEDS TALENT

ATTRACTING, EDUCATING & DEPLOYING

THE 21ST-CENTURY WORKFORCE

AMERICA NEEDS TALENT

RosettaBooks®

ATTRACTING, EDUCATING & DEPLOYING THE 21ˢᵗ-CENTURY WORKFORCE

JAMIE MERISOTIS

First edition published 2015 by RosettaBooks
Cover and interior design by Brehanna Ramirez

COVER IMAGES, TOP TO BOTTOM:

*Aerial view of downtown Dallas, Texas, by Robert Yarnall Richie courtesy of
DeGolyer Library, Central University Libraries, Southern Methodist
University*

*Photograph of Main Hall, US Immigration Station, Ellis Island ca. 1907–12
courtesy of Miriam and Ira D. Wallach Division of Art, Prints and Photographs,
New York Public Library*

*Aerial photograph of National Mall during William J. Clinton Presidential
Inauguration by Carl Hansen courtesy of Smithsonian Institution Archives*

*Space shuttle concept illustration courtesy of San Diego Air
& Space Museum Archives*

*Students and teacher in classroom at Cathedral High School in New Ulm,
Minnesota, by David Stroble courtesy of the US National Archives*

Library of Congress Control Number: 2015934056
ISBN-13: 978-0-7953-4592-0

www.RosettaBooks.com
Printed in the United States of America

For Colleen,
Benjamin and Elizabeth,
the most talented people I know.

CONTENTS

PART III. TALENT AND AMERICAN PROSPERITY

PROLOGUE

The book you are about to read is predicated on the notion that America's forward trajectory—its future prosperity—depends on the acquisition and development of talent.

As someone who has spent his career in the area of education generally and its advancement through philanthropy and public policy specifically, I often hear people say that education is the most important determinant of America's future. It's hard to argue with that—voluminous research shows that those who attain a high-quality education are almost always dramatically better off. It certainly was true in my case, coming from a family of limited means and no history of post–high school education. For the Merisotis family, like millions of other families, the education that my brothers and I received likely changed the economic and social course of an entire generation, ending a cycle that goes back to our rural village roots in Greece.

And yet I've often tried to articulate the fact that while education, particularly post–high school (or postsecondary) education, is without a doubt the most important investment choice we make in the United States, it's the *outcome* of education that is ultimately what matters most. It's not the systems that are important, nor the processes in and of themselves. Education, and related strategies like immigration and urban policy, are all aimed at helping both individuals and society bend a person's life trajectory toward something better. It's about talent, and how that talent is ultimately attracted, nurtured, and marshaled.

So, what is talent?

The term "talent" has been used in an infinite number of contexts, going back centuries. Indeed, history tells us that in ancient Greece, as well as in Rome and Egypt, "talent" signified a quantity of mass or value, often in gold or silver or some other precious metal. The Parable of the Talents, from Matthew 25:14–30, referred to this same monetary type of talent, but its reference to a servant who is given just one talent, while many more are buried in his backyard, can be extrapolated into our modern use of the word: a gift, or an ability that can benefit the common good.

The ability to benefit the common good has endured over the ages. Yet our idea of the common good may have changed somewhat since the ancients. In the United States, we tend to use "talent" to describe specific skills or capacities that an individual may have. In popular terms, talent has come to be known as something that a singer, dancer, athlete, or precocious child might possess. We often say someone is talented because that person has achieved a high level of success in a narrow space, and thus the ability to shine and prosper. Television shows, social media, and other popular communications tools all reinforce this notion.

America is full of that type of talent. But to me, talent is much more than that narrowly framed idea of a singular ability or skill. *Talent is a reflection of the synergies that result when individuals acquire a mix of capabilities that lead to prosperity in their careers and personal lives—synergies that not only impact them as individuals, but all of society.* Talent requires tacit knowledge, like a performance that's difficult to write down, visualize, or transfer directly from one person to another. It's an elusive mix of abilities that we can't easily categorize, like when we say Steve Jobs was "innovative," or when we discuss the complex mix of social skills we call "leadership."

In short, talent includes:

- *Knowledge*—understanding in a particular subject matter, such as math, science, or the humanities, as well as applied subjects like accounting.

- *Skills*—like critical thinking and problem solving, competencies that allow individuals to use their knowledge to solve problems as well as generate new knowledge.

- *Abilities*—like memory, creativity, and reasoning, enduring personal attributes that are innate to some extent, but can also be developed through formal and informal learning.

- *Values*—like recognition, achievement, and authority, preferences for outcomes, goals, or ideals.

- *Interests*—like social or investigative, the characteristics of the kinds of environments where people prefer to locate themselves.

- *Personality traits*—like conscientiousness or extroversion, habitual patterns of behavior, thought, or emotion that are relatively stable over time.

What follows is the story of how crucially important it is that we find, grow, and deploy American talent today and how we should go about doing it.

PART I

AMERICA'S TALENT CHALLENGE

1

THE AMERICAN CENTURY

In the February 17, 1941, edition of *Life*, Henry Luce, that magazine's publisher and a man who knew a thing or two about grand ambitions, argued against American isolationism and articulated a vision for the nation's role in the remainder of the 20th century. He opened starkly with this: "We Americans are unhappy. We are not happy about America. We are not happy about ourselves in relation to America. We are nervous—or gloomy—or apathetic." Then Luce then went on to make the case for optimism:

> Throughout the 17th Century and the 18th Century and the 19th Century, this continent

teemed with manifold projects and magnificent purposes. ...It is in this spirit that all of us are called, each to his own measure of capacity, and each in the widest horizon of his vision, to create the first great American Century.[1]

Luce's words were, of course, prophetic. The 20th century *was* the American Century. The isolationism he railed against gave way to a determined internationalist spirit that won World War II and liberated a continent in the process. The resulting boom in ingenuity, innovation, and accomplishment showed the world exactly what America was made of.

It was an era characterized by can-do spirit. When Franklin D. Roosevelt asked American industry to supply the necessary arsenal to rescue the Allies and defeat the Axis, business leaders created, in not much more than the blink of an eye, thousands of ships, planes, tanks, and guns, which won the war. Arthur Herman, in his history of the era, *Freedom's Forge*, recalled Adolph Hitler's sneering reaction to our entry into the conflict: "What is America but beauty queens, millionaires, stupid records, and Hollywood?"[2] Famous last words of a Führer.

President Roosevelt was physically decimated by the effects of polio, which he likely contracted during a vacation in Campobello Island off the coast of Maine in 1921.[3] Many today may be only vaguely familiar with the infectious disease, but in the first half of the 20th century, it killed or paralyzed millions, particularly infants and children. My mother was one of those people. An immigrant to the United States from Greece in the mid-1930s, she probably was infected with the disease growing up in the poor neighborhoods of Astoria, Queens, in New York City. She lived her life reasonably normally, but her experience and physical limitations were reminders to all of us in the Merisotis family that times were very different not so long ago.

By the 1950s, the virus had reached pandemic-like levels. In 1952, one of its most lethal outbreaks left over 3,000 dead and 21,000 infirmed.[4] The cure: American ingenuity and determination. Jonas Salk, a professor at the University of Pittsburgh, rallied his research team and relentlessly studied, tested, and experimented until they lit upon a remedy: a killed-virus vaccine, which virtually knocked the disease out, then and now. Polio cases are almost unheard of in America today, and are growing rarer around the world.[5]

Around this same time, both the United States and the Soviet Union began hurling rockets into outer space. The launch of the Sputnik spacecraft on October 4, 1957, made the Soviet Union the first nation with an artificial satellite in earth orbit. The communists had won the high ground in the Cold War and bragging rights in the race toward a high-technology future. Adding insult to injury, Americans could hear Sputnik chirping on the radio and many could see the tiny object in the sky in early morning and early evening as it traversed the United States every ninety-six minutes.

After the shock wore off, America's near-immediate and bipartisan reaction in 1958 was the National Defense Education Act (NDEA), a major federal investment in science and technology education. That same law also included the first-ever federal student assistance program, the National Defense Student Loans. That was a precursor to the significant federal investments that would follow in the Higher Education Act in 1965 (with the support of President Lyndon Johnson) and the Education Amendments of 1972 (with the support of President Richard Nixon).[6] Combined, these two laws were the basis for the current federal student aid system, which includes Pell Grants to support low-income student access to higher education, loans for students at all income levels, work-study, and numerous other programs.

By the 1960s, the rival superpowers were in a new race to see who could send the first human into space. The Russians got there first, again, when they launched Yuri Gagarin into earth orbit in April 1961. Next up was the race to see who could land on the moon itself. In September 1961, President John F. Kennedy doubled down on the space race, famously declaring, "We choose to go to the moon in this decade and do the other things, not because they are easy, but because they are hard, because that goal will serve to organize and measure the best of our energies and skills...."[7] A mere eight years later, Americans, in the form of the Apollo program, concluded a staggering feat of organizational prowess, scientific advancement, and human bravery by landing Neil Armstrong and Buzz Aldrin on the moon.

What is most surprising looking back is that these are just a few of the many astonishing accomplishments that characterized the American Century. We didn't just cure polio and win the race to the moon. We also helped raise Europe up from its postwar ashes, electrified every corner of the nation, put several cars in nearly every garage, gave many families a house to go with it, created and paved interconnected highways from coast to coast, won the Cold War, and created the Internet, which spawned many of the tech enterprises (Google, YouTube, Facebook) that are, at this point, central to our daily lives.

But how did a relatively young nation pull it off? Talent. That and a simple recipe that mixed four critical ingredients for developing and using talent:

1. *K–12 schools* that gave most Americans the basic education to allow them to sit on a jury and learn what they needed to know to make a lower-middle-class living;

2. *an elite higher education system* that produced rank-and-file professionals like school-teachers, lawyers, and accountants and also

produced top-notch Science, Technology, Engineering and Math (STEM) and managerial talent necessary to lead a global economic, technological, and military superpower;

3. *a set of uniquely American values* worthy of Jefferson's yeoman farmer and Horatio Alger's Ragged Dick: determination, democracy, individual initiative, and ingenuity; and

4. *a diverse demography and an expansive geography* that ensured robust debate about the best way to do just about anything, upsetting complacency and groupthink wherever it found a temporary safe haven in our workplaces, culture, or politics.

Talent reflects the amalgam of capabilities that lead to successes in personal lives and careers. That synergy goes beyond the individual, impacting society as well. As I will elaborate later in this book, talent is much more than innate ability: It is knowledge of particular domains and the human contexts that give it meaning. Knowledge without meaning is aimless and ineffectual. Talent is skill—the ability to use knowledge to learn more or solve problems. Talent is rooted in values: a deep belief in discovery, personal fulfillment, and service to others. And talent has a complicated personality: It is by turns conscientious, reflective, and engaged with others.

These are the raw ingredients in the recipe for talent mixed in innumerable ways in each of us. Talent is not born or bought; it is made, one person at a time, in supporting families and social institutions. Smart and efficient public policies also play a role in supporting the web of social institutions that nurture talent. In the American Century, we became open to diverse sources of talent and provided the social support necessary for its realization, giving us a nearly insurmountable advantage over our global competition. Big ideas capitalized on America's talents or allowed talented Americans to come up with their own big ideas. Look at college education, for example.

In the American Century, among our many accomplishments was a higher education system that became the best in the world. The Morrill Acts of 1862 and 1890 got the ball rolling by granting land to states for the creation of public universities.[8] Only a relatively small number of Americans attended college up until World War II.[9] Yet after the war, there were more veterans returning home than jobs waiting for them (the US actually staggered discharging veterans to avoid an employment crisis).

After World War I, a sickly President Wilson and an opposing Congress failed to put together a demobilization plan for those returning from the military. Among those who best remembered that failure were the members of concerned organizations such as the American Legion and the Veterans of Foreign Wars, soldiers who had served in that first Great War. They had returned home with far too little in the way of needed jobs and benefits. Their struggles inspired them to organize; when WWII ended, they were ready to lobby Congress to prepare a demobilization program to help transition America's soldiers back to civilian life. The product was written by Harry W. Colmery, a Topeka lawyer and Republican Party chair, in his room in Washington's Mayflower Hotel, and then brought to life by Senator Ernest McFarland (a Democrat) and Congresswoman Edith Nourse Rogers (a Republican). It was signed into law by President Roosevelt in 1944, formally known as the Servicemen's Readjustment Act.[10]

This piece of legislation, which we usually refer to as the GI Bill, provided the sixteen million returning veterans with tuition to any college or university of their choice. Eight million service men and women took Uncle Sam up on the offer, and flooded America's campuses. With the influx of new students—many of whom never had previous aspirations for college—these vibrant, teeming campuses in turn became the incubators of the talent that ushered in the space and information ages and turned the college degree into the key credential for job seekers for the remainder of the century. The GI Bill democratized the bachelor's degree and played a crucial role in establishing college as the preferred pathway into the American middle class.

And it wasn't just the returning American heroes who benefited from this recognition that a college diploma was essential to developing America's potential. The Higher Education Act, signed by President Lyndon Johnson in 1965, was premised on the idea that support for both low-income students and institutions of higher education advanced a critical national interest—expanding opportunities for more Americans to benefit from the knowledge and skills inherent in a college degree.[11] And the Civil Rights Act, passed the year before, helped create the conditions that enabled black, Latino, and other students to gain financial assistance and ensure admission to higher education.

Both pieces of legislation were milestones in the development of the American Century. Both acknowledged that opportunity needs to continually expand to include new groups, to ensure equity for all those with the motivation and drive to succeed. These steps were not driven by *noblesse oblige*, but instead by what was for a long time a uniquely American view that our prosperity and way of life depended on expanding the pool of talent. Indeed, phrases like "the American dream" and "land of opportunity" were often used to describe this era, a time when we knew that we had to be a country that did more than serve its elites well and hope that others might benefit indirectly from that success.

The American Century also provided a happy ending to a story close to my own heart. The century saw the fulfillment of the hopes of Eastern and Southern European ethnics who came in waves early in the 20th century. This included people with names like Russo, Cohen, Papadopoulos, Kowalski, and numerous others in search of better lives than the economically moribund and socially stagnant ones they had left behind. The welcome mat was out briefly for them early in the century and they rushed in. They had fully "arrived" in America only when the door to higher education opened, and their children and grandchildren fulfilled their parents' and grandparents' version of the American dream.

Throughout the history of the country, Americans have disputed who should come across our borders and in what numbers. The 20th century was no different, especially when those from Eastern Europe and Italy supplanted German and English immigrants in the first few decades of the 1900s. An immigration restriction act, limiting the number of immigrants per nation to 2 percent of their fellow countrymen already in the United States, was passed in 1924.[12] Laws such as these were driven by prejudice toward the new class of immigrants—many of whom came across the Atlantic in search of employment or to escape war or religious persecution—but they were often ineffective. Millions of Italians, Jews, Slavs, and Greeks immigrated to the States before the Great Depression. Not all of them remained or even assimilated, but this influx of new citizens undoubtedly played an essential role in the heavy lifting of powering America's economic growth in the 20th century and broadening of our culture, particularly in urban areas.

And the glue that held it all together, from the GIs returning home, to the minorities striving for the rights promised in our founding documents, to the children and grandchildren of the Eastern and Southern European ethnics, was a unifying belief in *the idea* of America: a place where hard work and self-determination reaped rewards; where civic engagement and faith in our institutions played a vital role in citizenship; and where our leaders, armed with unshakeable confidence in the idea of America, inspired millions to do great things.

Let's go back to the moon for a moment. When President Kennedy took the podium at Rice University in the late summer of 1961 to challenge the nation to literally reach for the stars, NASA barely had even the building blocks of the technology and equipment necessary for such an endeavor.

Think of it. Space and its exploration had been contemplated since the time of the ancient Greeks— indeed, as early as 190 AD, the rhetorician Lucian of Samosata wrote of man departing for the cosmos. An American president challenged his nation, which had little to none of the necessary hardware, to land a man on the moon in a decade. And it did just that. Because we believed, because we had the American people, and they had the talent.

This can-do attitude and faith in the human talents among us gave Americans a nearly insurmountable advantage over our global competition in all fields. We won world wars, we cured incurable diseases, and we generated awe-inspiring technology. And along the way, Henry Luce became a bit of a prophet.

But it's worth considering in the early years of the 21st century: Do we still have the skills we need, do we still believe, can we still muster the talent to do it all again?

2

A NATION AT RISK

As a prelude to his State of the Union address in January 2004, President George W. Bush served up an imposing challenge: The United States, he boldly proposed, should put a man on Mars as early as 2030, and return our astronauts to the moon in sixteen years. "Mankind is drawn to the heavens for the same reason we were once drawn into unknown lands and across the open sea. We choose to explore space because doing so improves our lives and lifts our national spirit," Bush reasoned, in words that echoed President Kennedy's from nearly half a century earlier.[13]

Born in 1964, I am too young to remember Kennedy's inspiring words. But I do recall the speech that President Bush gave. I thought it was a bold stroke for a president facing what was at the time daunting re-election prospects. As a policy analyst and researcher who had made his career in Washington, DC, up until that point, I had the privilege of witnessing a fair amount of bipartisan—indeed sometimes cross-national—inspirational collaboration in federal policy. For instance, I recall the amazing confluence of events in 1987 that led a cold warrior president, Ronald Reagan, to welcome the Soviet president, Mikhail Gorbachev, to Washington, with the enthusiastic commitment of Americans and their political leaders from all political persuasions. That summit was a prelude to the events of a few years later, when Gorbachev made historic decisions that ultimately ended the Soviet Union. Americans were unified in their support for the efforts to help the Soviet Union transform.

And I remember the fascinating way that, in 1996, President Bill Clinton was able to pull off the most comprehensive reform of federal welfare benefits in decades,[14] even though he was personally embroiled in controversy (and even though the merits of the success of his Personal Responsibility and Work Opportunity Reconciliation Act are still being debated). Clinton saw beyond the confines of party and ideology to pursue changes to a system desperately in need of reform, one where support for self-improvement via work, education, and training might create a more permanent change in the life circumstances of those the programs were intended to serve.

Even in my own small slice of the world, I had found some measure of reasoned compromise and collaboration. In 1991, as executive director of the National Commission on Responsibilities for Financing Postsecondary Education, a bipartisan federal commission tasked with rethinking the federal role in financing postsecondary education, I worked with a diverse group of politically appointed commissioners charged with addressing the growing challenge of college affordability at a time of fiscal stringency. It was a resonant echo of today's nearly identical but far more urgent discussions.

The National Commission was authorized by legislation written by Senator James Jeffords of Vermont, best known for his 2001 decision to abandon the Republican Party and become an independent. Jeffords' decision rocked Washington at the time, because it cost Republicans the majority in the Senate and left his friend President George W. Bush in an awkward and challenging set of circumstances.[15] A lifelong Republican and descendant of a family of Republican leaders in the state, Jeffords made a political choice based on principle, putting his convictions and beliefs above ideology and party. As Jeffords observed in his 2001 memoir *My Declaration of Independence*, "I had to be true to what I thought was right, and leave the consequences to sort themselves out in the days ahead."[16]

The National Commission, formed a decade earlier, reflected that same kind of independent, do-what's-right attitude. Commission members, who were appointed by both the president and congressional leaders, represented the full spectrum of political views—right, center, and left. The five Republicans and four Democrats on the panel spent two years studying and debating the causes of and potential government solutions to the lack of college affordability. The commission's final report, "Making College Affordable Again," ended up as headline news in 1993, and is a testament to the hard work and reasonable compromise that defined the participants as a group.[17] It was a unanimous report—no minority dissent or exceptional explanation was included in the report—and was called bold and forward-looking. Several of the commission's recommendations became federal policy under Presidents Clinton, Bush, and Obama, while others never did make it into law.

Much has been written about the striking social changes that were experienced between the early 1990s—the very earliest days of the public Internet—and the mid-2000s. Perhaps the world really was simpler in those times. Whatever the reasons, I have often thought about whether we would be able to pull off a unanimous vote on the same final report today.

President Bush's return to space speech, delivered a decade after my own fifteen minutes of fame with the National Commission report, was not as well received as I and perhaps others had hoped. The symmetry between two presidents' words—one made during the Cold War stresses of the early 1960s, the other made during the fearful and uncertain post-9/11 world—is striking. But their receptions could not have been more dissimilar. An Associated Press poll taken after Bush's 2004 speech revealed that the majority of Americans felt the resources necessary for such an endeavor would be better spent elsewhere.[18]

Now, if you're worried that you accidently bought a book on space policy in America, don't despair: I am not a rocket scientist and this is not a treatise on the future of NASA. But these two presidential speeches, their proposals, their receptions, and their aftermaths provide useful metaphors. We are in a new century, facing new challenges and new, often unpleasant, realities.

The old formula, the one that helped make the American Century, doesn't quite add up anymore. And there is no guarantee that the successes of the 1900s will be repeated—at least not on our shores.

The topic of American decline has been debated, affirmed, debunked, and studied quite a bit in recent years. I won't dwell on decline here; the subject's been covered by more books than I can count. For our purposes, it's better to look at America's place in the world in the early part of the 21st century with regard to where we stand in a global competition: a competition for innovation, investment, growth, and prosperity, and, above all else, the key to creating those—talent.

The truth is, here in the early decades of the 21st century, we are at real risk of falling behind in this contest. Our advantages from the past century are either irrelevant or in jeopardy. Let's take a look:

Public education in America, despite billions of dollars' worth of investments and the best efforts of educators as well as reformers from all parts of the political spectrum, is frankly, abysmal. Survey after survey shows our system lagging behind. In 2012, a collaborative study by the education firm Pearson and *The Economist* placed America's K–12 schools seventeenth in the developed world—behind such countries as Belgium, Singapore, and Canada.[19] A separate study conducted by scholars at Harvard, Stanford, and the University of Munich showed that US test scores are falling behind those of another set of nations including Latvia and Chile.[20] Let me repeat that: Latvia and Chile.

Our vaunted higher education system also is in the midst of a crisis of confidence. Americans increasingly doubt the value of the college degree, once the preferred path toward employment and entrance to the middle class. Rising tuition fees and soaring student debt, coupled with confusion about the employment prospects of graduates—especially those coming from schools with a poor track record of producing graduates with high-quality educations and useful skills—have led some to even conclude that higher education has become a futile pursuit.

This doctrine could not be more wrong or more poorly timed. Here's why: According to the Georgetown Center on Education and the Workforce, fifty-five million new jobs will be created by the end of this decade. Of these, forty million—more than 70 percent—will require a college-level certificate or degree. And by 2020, the center says, 65 percent of *all* US jobs will require a postsecondary credential. But according to census figures, less than 40 percent of Americans hold at least an associate degree; another 5 percent hold a certificate or other nondegree credential.[21] These numbers reveal a significant gap between current postsecondary (or "college," since I believe these terms are interchangeable) attainment and future needs—at a time when Gallup and other polling firms are showing that Americans are increasingly seeing higher education as the most important path to high-quality jobs.

In fact, the majority of new jobs already *require* postsecondary education. If you need a concrete example of that, visit your local auto repair shop. A generation ago, nearly two-thirds of America's car mechanics were high school dropouts. Today, more than a third have attended college.

In other words, America needs talent now more than ever, but Americans aren't yet fully grasping that college is the best way to ensure that supply of talent.

Addressing this gap has become a clarion call for my professional work over the past two decades. When I arrived at Lumina Foundation as its CEO in 2008, the foundation already was doing impressive work around increasing college access and success. As I began to find my way as the leader of one of the nation's largest private foundations—a unique entity because of its large asset base combined with a tightly focused mission—it dawned on us that the foundation had an opportunity to do more than just be a good grant-making organization. We had the opportunity to be a different kind of entity, a leadership organization—an opportunity that I hope we are fulfilling to this day.

The founding members of Lumina's board made a conscious and courageous decision to keep Lumina's mission homed on just one issue: increasing college access and success, especially for low-income, first-generation, and other underserved populations. For an organization with as much financial capacity as Lumina—a private foundation with an endowment well in excess of a billion dollars—that decision was almost unprecedented. Blessed with significant resources, very few large foundations tend to apply them in just one area, and many choose to address several issues with different investment strategies, all simultaneously. The Lumina board's initial decision to devote the foundation's mission entirely to increasing postsecondary attainment has imprinted all we do.

And yet we concluded that in order to truly fulfill that mission, we had to be specific. We crafted a different approach, one that has set us apart both in higher education and philanthropy. We chose to set a time-limited, quantified goal for all of our work, whether it be grantmaking, or working to support effective public policy, or just trying to influence the national dialogue in a way that would result in real, system-level change. The goal—ensuring that 60 percent of Americans hold a high-quality post-secondary degree, certificate, or other credential by the year 2025—was based on the projections that the Georgetown Center had done showing how big of a gap the US had to narrow in order to address its talent needs. It was also triangulated with the fact that many of our global competitors had already blown past the US attainment rate of 40 percent, and in a few cases (like Korea and Canada) had already surpassed that 60 percent goal.[22] Today, leaders from President Obama to governors from both parties to college leaders have embraced this goal, or one very similar to it.

The goal is fundamentally a means to an end: Increasing the proportion of Americans with high-quality postsecondary education qualifications will add enormously to the talent base of the country. But for many in the US, the opportunities available to narrow those talent gaps are few, especially based on students' race and income. The Georgetown Center recently reported that, between 1994 and 2008, 68 percent of African-American college student enrollment and 72 percent of new Hispanic enrollment was at open-admission four-year colleges and two-year colleges. Over the same period, 82 percent of new white student enrollment was at the 464 most selective four-year colleges.[23]

Of course, admissions selectivity doesn't guarantee high quality, and open-admissions policies don't necessarily eliminate rigor. Still, it's hard to ignore the reality here: By and large, American students are traveling on separate postsecondary pathways, divergent pathways that lead to unequal educational opportunities and outcomes—a lower level of talent than what we need for the nation's collective well-being, not just for their future as individuals.

Meanwhile, the world's most rapidly developing economies are leading the way in innovations to education. In other words, innovation thrives most where education and employment are tightly intertwined. In the year 2000, according to the Organization for Economic Cooperation and Development, ninety-one million young adults worldwide had a college education. Of this number, 17 percent each were from the US and China, 12 percent were from Russia, and 10 percent each were from Japan and India.[24]

However, based on projections for 2020, we will see a dramatic shift in the countries that are leading in postsecondary attainment. Of the world's 200 million young adults who are expected to hold post-secondary degrees by 2020, 42 percent will come from two countries—China, with 30 percent, and India, with 12 percent—while the US share of the world's college graduates is expected to decline to 11 percent.[25]

At the same time, the inflow of immigrants, a major contribution to the mind and muscle that made the American Century, is being redirected. President Obama threw down the gauntlet in late 2014 on immigration reform, using the tool of executive action to move on what he saw as unacceptable inaction by Congress, especially focused on the millions of people living in the US undocumented and facing challenging work and life prospects.[26] Whatever one's views of the merits of the president's executive order, it still leaves the country far short of where it needs to be. At this writing, Congress is struggling to make progress on even the most basic and common-sense immigration reforms, instead focusing its energy and ire on defining the limits of the executive powers of a president.

Despite howls of protest from business and thought leaders from across the political spectrum—even Sheldon Adelson, Warren Buffett, and Bill Gates agree on this—the prospects are bleak for any sort of meaningful change that is wide-ranging and will have a lasting impact on the nation's talent deficits.[27] In contrast to our most recent effort at a comprehensive immigration overhaul, which went down in flames in

2007,[28] we may get some cobbled-together legislation that nibbles around the edges of a serious national problem in need of a truly grand fix. Or, given the enduring contemporary dysfunction on the Potomac, we may not get anything.

Either way, while Washington bickers and fiddles, our global competitors, like sharp human resource managers, are luring away talented men and women who might otherwise arrive on our shores, using smarter and simpler laws—laws that might even (and this is the kicker) attract Americans who figure they will have an easier time starting a business abroad. Spain, for example, has made a hard play for foreign talent at the high end of the spectrum, recently passing a law that has resulted in a boom in entrepreneurialism and new business development.[29]

Writing in *The Wall Street Journal*, Steve Case, the cofounder of America Online, pointed out in distressing detail that Germany, Australia, China, and Canada have all recently adjusted their immigration laws to attract and retain entrepreneurs, while America struggles to do the same. "Will we see America's advantage move overseas?" Case asks.[30] It's a good question. And its answer will impact millions of native-born Americans as well. According to the Americas Society and the Council of the Americas, an annual influx of 100,000 immigrants would create 46,000 jobs and generate $80 billion in housing wealth.[31]

It is clear that America's edge and the prosperity it brings are in peril until we recognize that our immigration debate should not be about whom we want within our borders or where they come from, but rather what type of society we want and how we recruit the talent to help construct it.

American ethos, the third part of our previously unbeatable equation from the past century, is less quantifiable or easily measured. But we have enough anecdotal evidence to suspect this too may be deteriorating.

Make no mistake: Americans have never had a Pollyannaish love of their government, or a blind trust in all their institutions. Yes, our founders bequeathed us a healthy suspicion toward those we entrust with power and realistic expectations about what the state can do to foster human happiness. But through the years, Americans have understood that success comes from a balanced mix of hard work, self-sufficiency, and observation of the law of equal success, or as we often call it, the American dream. But for this to work, we also must place some level of trust in our institutions and the elected officials who oversee them in order to make sure that the playing field remains level and effort is justifiably rewarded.

Yet as we continue to lurch uneasily and unevenly out of the Great Recession, and scores of jobs have disappeared, never to return, many Americans are losing faith. Losing faith that their hard work will be rewarded, losing faith in their leaders, and losing faith in their institutions.

In 2012, *National Journal* published a disturbing essay, written by Ron Fournier and Sophie Quinton, "In Nothing We Trust." The piece charted the foreclosed homes, lost jobs, and obstructive city halls that characterized the postrecession era. "Seven in 10 Americans believe that the country is on the wrong track; eight in 10 are dissatisfied with the way the nation is being governed. Only 23 percent have confidence in banks, and just 19 percent have confidence in big business. Less than half the population expresses 'a great deal' of confidence in the public school system or organized religion," they reported.[32]

A more recent study by the federal Corporation for National and Community Service found that civic engagement through volunteerism and engagement with community organizations has waned, with declines in four out of five civic engagement indicators measured by the agency.[33] And if you wonder why Americans might be less inspired by their leaders these days, just look at all the indictments, convictions, or resignations of those leaders, or at the tweets of various elected officials and office seekers—actually don't look at those tweets; this is a PG-rated book.

The 2014 midterm elections, which saw a Republican takeover of the US Senate after an eight-year hiatus, added to this miserable view. The election was not exactly a ringing endorsement from the public about the current slate of political leaders, or virtually anything else. Exit polls from that election showed that voters were disgruntled with just about everything, from the economy, to the two political parties, to the direction of the country.[34]

Now you might be asking yourself what, exactly, does this have to do with talent? It's all related and it's all cyclical. Part of the reason so many Americans have stopped believing is that so many have been out of work for so long, or have given up on any sort of meaningful increase in their quality of life. At the time of this writing, unemployment in America is hovering around 6 percent, an improvement from 10 percent in October 2009. But more important than the rate is this: The number of Americans in the labor market—working or looking for a job—has shriveled to a thirty-five-year low. Indeed, nearly ten million Americans were still unemployed in late 2014. But employers are unable to fill more than two million jobs. Why? Lack of knowledge, skills, and abilities: in a word, talent.

We need a bout of growth to create jobs and put those Americans back to work. And with the economy so radically changed over the past decade, we also need a new wave of innovation to grow new jobs in new sectors. We need talented innovators, from both here and abroad, to help create that, and we need a 21st-century education system to train citizens to hold those jobs.

It should be noted that an education system that is failing students or turning them away doesn't just hinder us in this global competition; it also corrodes our society. Schools, both K–12 and throughout higher education, prepare young people for citizenship and civic life, to hold jobs, to contribute to society, and to think objectively. If students are not being properly educated in our public school system or being told they needn't bother with college, how do we expect them to embrace those American ideas or put faith in our system and its institutions?

Back to the cosmos one last time. President Bush's proposed mission to Mars, "The Vision for Space Exploration," was canned in 2010 and replaced with a considerably more modest proposal. Many commentators argued that the scaling back of the space program and the new policy's growing collaboration with the private sector was actually a step in the right direction, and a necessary one given America's strained resources. This may well be. But the more recent facts are ominous. Compare the failure of an early mission of Virgin Galactic, the most touted of the private space ventures, when its vehicle broke apart in flight in late 2014, to the success of the European Space Agency's (ESA) feat of landing a spacecraft on a three-mile-wide comet roughly 300 million miles from earth just a few weeks later. In fact, the declining prominence of the US in this arena gave the head of the ESA, Jean-Jacques Dordain, an opportunity for some in-your-face braggadocio. "Today, we have demonstrated that the European expertise—be it at ESA, be it in industry, in national space agencies, in research centers—everywhere, this is the best expertise of the world," the Frenchman gloated. "Because we are the *first* to have done that. And that will stay forever!"[35]

In the most recent century, both by choice and out of necessity, America was often the first to accomplish many things. We achieved great, grand outcomes, and we had the talent to do so. We will need to do these things again in the 21st century. Whether we are capable of doing so is an open question.

3

WINNING THE FUTURE

We've surveyed the past and assessed the present. Now let's turn to the future. We know that America's traditional advantages have ebbed, that friendly (and not-so-friendly) competitors have not only achieved parity with us but also are beginning to surpass the US when it comes to creating tomorrow's jobs and attracting and preparing workers to fill them.

The consequences? Well, the Organization for Economic Cooperation and Development (them again) reported in early 2013 that, by 2016, China's economy would replace America's as the Number 1 in the world.[36] Barely eighteen months later, a report from the International Monetary Fund said that that replacement quite possibly had already happened.[37] Now, I am not an office holder or seeker, so I can be frank and say that being Number 2, while not something we would seek out, probably isn't the end of the world. But it is evidence of a larger trend: an indication that the dynamism that fueled our prosperity in the previous century is dissipating here and materializing elsewhere, an assertion supported by the fact that over half of all the patents awarded by the US government since 2008 have gone to innovators from other countries.

And this trend will come with costs beyond slipping a place or two in global economic rankings. If we are not producing a new generation of innovators, thinkers, educators, and entrepreneurial daredevils, we are likely to see a sharp slide in our overall quality of life here in America.

Many leaders from different perspectives share this view. Mohamed El-Erian is certainly one of them. El-Erian is senior adviser at Allianz and best known for his prior executive role at PIMCO, the nation's largest manager of fixed-income securities like bonds, and as the head of Harvard Management Co., which manages the endowment and pension assets of Harvard University. We met at a dinner in 2014, where the topic was how to improve social mobility, and it led to an interesting discussion about how talent fits into this question of quality of life in the US.

Unsurprisingly, El-Erian chalked much of the current crisis up to improper investment. Americans, he believes, have spent the past ten years growing in all the wrong ways. "A decade ago we lost sight of our growth model; we fell in love with the wrong concept of growth," he lamented. "We stopped investing wisely, and as a result fell behind in education and infrastructure. We have not invested in the engines of sustainable growth."

El-Erian, who also serves on President Obama's Global Development Council, has been a bit of a Cassandra since the Great Recession, warning that the high unemployment and low wages that accompanied the downturn could very well turn into a new normal long after recovery is complete. And without a more robust system of talent development, there may be no real recovery in sight. "Six years after the recession, we still have high long-term unemployment, a low participation rate, high teenage unemployment," he warns. "The longer this persists, the harder it will be to bounce back."

And it's not just about dollars and cents. Wide-ranging social and cultural implications are attached to this new, less-prosperous normal. Yes, in the 20th century we liberated a continent, cured previously incurable diseases, sent men to the moon, became the world's primary manufacturer, and ushered in the Internet age. But our preeminence was not just produced in labs, factories, or in Silicon Valley. Our amalgamated culture, as vibrant and vast as our landscapes, as diverse and imaginative as our population, was the world's culture.

The motion picture industry was raised and perfected in Hollywood and then exported around the world. Like nearly every facet of our country, it was propelled by immigrants: Rudolph Valentino, Charlie Chaplin, and Cary Grant all passed through Ellis Island on their way to Tinseltown. Today, the industry, according to the likes of Steven Spielberg and George Lucas, is on the verge of a technology-driven "implosion" while film industries grow in India, China, and South Korea. In fact, in the spring of 2013 the Chinese government unveiled the Beijing International Screenwriting Competition, an initiative to lure American writers and wannabes to its burgeoning cinema industry.[38]

Our cultural dominance was aural as well. Jazz, blues, rock 'n' roll, pop, and other indigenous sounds are a part of our cultural currency and were played all over the world. Other nations, such as Britain, got in on the act, but think about the reach of our influence: Kids in Liverpool (the Beatles) and London (the Rolling Stones) huddled around their turntables studying and then copying music made by a sharecropper's son from Tiptonville, Tennessee (Carl Perkins), or a bluesman from Jug's Corner, Mississippi (Muddy Waters). Today, American (and British) kids are downloading and dancing to pop songs recorded in Seoul and rapped in Korean.

How about the Prague-born playwright/freedom fighter/president Vaclav Havel? His battle to rid the former Czechoslovakia of communism was inspired by American artists such as Frank Zappa and the Lou Reed–led Velvet Underground. In the 1980s and 1990s, rap and hip-hop artists helped shape American culture, though most of it was hardly revolutionary. More recently, it's difficult to see who might have even that kind of influence. Are we currently producing any artists who will inspire future revolutionaries? Kim Kardashian?

Now lest we be accused of protectionism, it should be said that there is nothing at all wrong with cultural interchange. Americans *should* be listening to and enjoying the arts of other cultures. But it is a sign that even our cultural influence is waning, and other nations are doing what we used to do and possibly doing it better. Jazz, for example, an American-born and -bred invention, has improbably found a new home in nations on several different continents, with accomplished artists who are feted around the globe. People like Igor Butman, a Russian saxophonist who has made a name as one of the world's leading jazz innovators, and Dhafer Youssef, a Tunisian composer and singer.

Or take a look at the rosters of most teams in Major League Baseball. You are increasingly likely to see names such as Tanaka, Cabrera, and Ryu. Or NBA basketball teams dominated by people named Nowitzki, Ginobili, and Antetokounmpo. These are not immigrants, who have strengthened our social and economic capacities in innumerable ways. These are foreign nationals, who are coming to the US and doing what Americans traditionally have done well, but increasingly are doing it *better*. Again, there's nothing sinister about ball players coming to America to ply their trade, but it's obvious that other countries are producing something very important at a much quicker clip than we are: talent.

The horizons are ominous: Forty-seven million Americans are living in poverty.[39] Median household income has actually declined since the 1990s.[40] Read the paper, surf the web, or just talk to friends and family, and you will increasingly hear depressing and foreboding terms such as "lost generation," "quit looking for work," "jobs aren't coming back." Jim Clifton, CEO of Gallup, predicts a coming global war for jobs. If that's the case, we are about to take an ill-equipped army that skipped out on basic training to the battlefield, where they will face well-trained fighting forces with all the latest military technology. A Springfield 1861 vs. a Super Aegis 2.

Because so many young Americans are not armed with the tools necessary to compete in the 21st century, we are failing to launch new generations in the transition from dependent youth to independent adulthood and successful family formation. New economic realities have changed the traditional life cycle of learning, work, and retirement, lengthening the time it takes for young people to settle into a career. Moreover, no longer are the relationships among education, work, and retirement strictly linear.

Over the past three decades, the median age at which young workers reach financial independence has increased from twenty-six to thirty; for young African-Americans, the age has increased to thirty-three.[41] The new knowledge economy has created a new phase in the transition from youth dependency to adult independence. Many young Americans are now struggling to become independent.

- Only one out of three adults in their early twenties and just over half of adults in their late twenties are employed in full-time jobs.[42]

- Young adults' labor force participation rate has returned to its 1972 level, a decline that started in the late 1990s and accelerated beginning in 2000.[43]

One result of these trends, in combination with the Great Recession, has been a lost decade for young people, marked by declining access to full-time jobs. Between 2000 and 2012, the employment rate for young people fell from 84 percent to 72 percent. It has been especially difficult for:

- young men, whose rate of full-time employment fell from 80 to 65 percent;[44]

- young adults with no education past high school, whose employment fell from 66 percent to 53 percent;[45] and

- young African-Americans, whose peak postrecession unemployment rate was 30 percent, twice as high as that of young whites.[46]

Future prospects for young adults may be compromised further by a generational imbalance in resources between young and old. Between 1970 and 2010, Medicare and Social Security nearly doubled as a share of public spending (from 12 percent to 23 percent[47]), while spending on education and training programs fell from 19 percent to 15 percent of public spending.[48]

As a result of increasing human capital requirements, the education and labor market institutions that were the foundation of the 20th-century industrial system are out of sync with the 21st-century economy.

The first step to a modernized system of work and learning is greater transparency in the alignment between postsecondary programs and career pathways. In addition, young adults will need to mix work and learning at earlier stages in the on-ramp to careers.

Stepping back from all the data and metaphors, let's put it this way: The jobs of the 21st century require 21st-century education, and we are doing a fairly lousy job of providing it to our work-force-in-waiting. As a consequence, employment opportunities are going elsewhere. And homegrown positions will soon be fewer and farther between. As they go, so goes our quality of life and our global position: American world leadership will be forfeited if we don't have the world's most gifted society. If we are not *the* cutting edge, our standing declines, and so will our standard of living. If that happens, America will run the risk of being a nation of also-rans, one out of many countries stuck in the pack. The thinkers, builders, inventors, and educators, the immigrant culture builders, all so essential to our character and prosperity, will flower in foreign soil. "We're Number 2!" isn't really a catchy slogan. But it might be the best we can do.

There's no shortage of suggestions of what America needs to avert this fate. Here's mine:

America *needs* talent.

This, more than anything, must be our goal in these early years of the 21st century: to build a society endowed with the skills, smarts, and drive to keep pace with the progress unfolding all around us—rapidly changing economies, quickly adapting and evolving global competitors—and, by doing so, ensure another century of prosperity.

This is our greatest challenge, and our ability to meet it will determine the destiny of the country. That's because the strength of our nation—or any nation—is its people, the sum total of knowledge, skills, and abilities inherent in the citizenry. And only with sufficient talent, and the right kinds of talent, can we meet the demands of this new era.

Talent development and deployment, then, must be America's prime objective. It's an objective that I firmly believe we can meet. America has faced greater challenges in its past, and the raw materials needed to rise to the occasion are at our disposal.

Now, the hard part. How *do* we harness and grow our existing talent? And how *do* we do a better job of attracting talent from elsewhere that can meet our current and future needs?

Elected officials and thought leaders have suggested all sorts of policy prescriptions to get the country back on track, but I believe it can be done through a simple set of ideas. Five ideas, in fact. Ideas that I have formulated for years, as a first-generation college graduate and American raised in an immigrant family, as the head of a bipartisan federal commission and cofounder of a nonpartisan think tank (the Institute for Higher Education Policy), and as the CEO of Lumina Foundation, the nation's largest private endowment dedicated to championing higher education attainment. These are collaborative solutions, created with input and support from employers, thought leaders, and everyday people. Taken together, they form a strategy to redesign the postsecondary education system, find the new workers we will so urgently need, crack the political stalemate and policy drought in Washington, and revive American innovation.

The Five Ways to attract, educate, and deploy talent begin with rethinking the nation's most important system for talent development: higher education. In the new system, learning will have to be the most important outcome of the system, not how much time students spent in a classroom, and not which school they attended.

Second, we need to unleash private sector innovation in ways that encourage risk-taking that will yield enormous benefits for our talent infrastructure in the coming years.

Third, we need to rethink, consolidate, and repurpose the federal role in talent development and deployment, putting in place an entirely new structure created from the good but uncoordinated work of disparate agencies.

Fourth, we need to develop a new immigration model built around the type of talent we need to create the society we want to live in—and we need to learn how other nations have done just that.

And fifth, we need to reimagine our cities as hubs of talent, where innovation and commerce thrive to fuel the talent fires in new ways.

These ideas are more than a laundry list of suggestions. They cut across the typical lines of ideology, system, or perspective. At this time of great anxiety and uncertainty for the nation, we desperately need new and better ideas.

I believe that the new and better ideas presented here are the natural enemy of the way things are. It's not Yorktown, Gettysburg, or Normandy, but this quest to find and implement ideas for making America more talented is a pivotal engagement. And the success of our battle plan will define the economic and social well-being of our democracy for decades to come.

It won't be easy, but the future is actually quite winnable. The following chapters explain how.

4

TALENT, YOU SAY?

In ancient times, a "talent" was a measurement of weight, and, by extension, the value of that weight in gold or silver. Even then, talent was valuable and desirable.

Given that this book is predicated on the notion that America's forward trajectory—its future prosperity—depends on the acquisition and development of talent, it's only reasonable to reiterate exactly what *I* mean by talent. That may help contextualize the Five Ways to attract, educate, and deploy talent that are the framing for this book.

So, what is talent? And who is talented? Is it something we are born with? Or is it something inherent in humans that, given the right circumstances, can be cultivated? Do some humans spring forth with the ability to achieve greatness in their chosen endeavors while others get left out in the cold, destined for a life of mediocrity?

It's hard to talk about talent without first discussing competencies: the knowledge, skills, abilities, values, interests, and personality traits that people need to live fully in their time. As noted earlier, talent is a reflection of the synergies that result when individuals acquire a mix of capabilities that lead to prosperity in their careers and personal lives—synergies that impact not only them as individuals, but all of society.

There's lots of academic research on this subject. Let me try to boil it down to a few core concepts for our purposes. Knowledge, skills, and abilities (KSAs) represent the core cognitive dimensions to talent:

- *Knowledge* is understanding in a particular subject matter, such as math, science, or the humanities, as well as applied subjects like accounting.

- *Skills*, like critical thinking and problem solving, are competencies that allow individuals to use their knowledge to solve problems as well as generate new knowledge.

- *Abilities*, like memory, creativity, and reasoning, are enduring personal attributes that are innate, to some extent, but can also be developed through formal and informal learning.

Values, interests, and personality traits are the non-cognitive dimensions to talent:

- *Values*, like recognition, achievement, and authority, are preferences for outcomes, goals, or ideals.

- *Interests*, like social or investigative, are the characteristics of the kinds of environments where people prefer to locate themselves.

- *Personality traits*, like conscientiousness or extroversion, are habitual patterns of behavior, thought, or emotion that are relatively stable over time.

Traditionally, economists and educators emphasized the importance of the cognitive dimensions to talent. But recent research demonstrates that personality traits can be as important as KSAs in determining educational and career success.

Gallup is one organization doing research in this context. We often think of Gallup in association with political polling and quality of life studies, but the CEO, Jim Clifton, is recognized as a bit of a savant when it comes to identifying and developing talent. In fact, the organization itself partners with companies to help identify, recruit, and nurture talent. In Gallup's somewhat unique perspective, talent can be broken down into two categories: innate and inherent abilities, and those than can be cultivated through training and education.

Gallup's research focuses on the psychology of innovators. Through testing and measurement, they find out what's under the hood, so to speak, to identify the areas where individuals excel, and what is best suited to their abilities, in terms of occupation and labor. Gallup's reasoning is that businesses and societies as a whole benefit from happy workers, people enjoying their work and excelling at it.

Gallup's Washington, DC, offices symbolically look out onto the Old Patent Office Building, where American talent was formally recognized for many decades. One fall afternoon, I sat in a Gallup conference room and asked Clifton and other members of his leadership team what exactly *is* talent and how vital is it to our country's well-being.

"Because we live in a knowledge economy, gone are the days when natural resources was the base of our economy," says Sangeeta Bharadwaj-Badal, an Indian-born PhD who has studied and written extensively about the psychology of innovators and what internal factors make for successful business leaders. As a senior leader at Gallup, she has interviewed thousands of entrepreneurs, analyzed their behaviors and actions, and concluded that risk-taking, initiative, and creativity—the abilities we associate with innovation—are often innate. Society's task is to help develop those talents, especially in a slumping global economy.

"With the economic recession we have seen around the world, Gallup has offered a solution by helping leverage the inherent human capital in an economy and using that to move the economy," she says. "If we focus on developing human potential, the returns are going to be much higher."

The inherent talents theory makes some sense. It's hard to argue, for example, that Georgia O'Keeffe, Wolfgang Amadeus Mozart, or Miles Davis were not given some sort of inherent upper hand on all other artists, composers, or trumpeters. And there is no doubt some truth to that. Talent shows up in individuals with characteristics not unlike a fingerprint: Some common features and patterns say something about who you are, but each is unique. And yet there is clearly more to it than that. Chas Chandler, who managed and cultivated Jimi Hendrix, once remarked that though Hendrix clearly had a brain geared toward understanding his instrument, it took countless hours, days, and years of practice to realize the music and guitar pyrotechnics Hendrix is remembered for.[49]

In a broad review of talent and how it is produced, in the best-selling *Outliers: The Story of Success*, Malcolm Gladwell examines the factors that contribute to high levels of success in sports, business, academe, and entertainment. His essential conclusion is summed up in his "10,000-Hour Rule," suggesting that the key to success in any field is complex, but essentially a matter of practice, practice, practice. Whether you want to be the next Jimi Hendrix or the next Larry Ellison, the ante in the game is a minimum of 10,000 hours of focused learning (twenty hours for fifty weeks a year for ten years) just to become a competent entrepreneur or a pretty good guitarist. Gladwell's 10,000-hour rule is a catchy journalistic summary that popularized the work on talent by people such as the Nobel laureate Herbert Simon and K. Anders Ericsson. It is long since a settled matter that instruments like IQ tests that measure innate ability are limited in their capacity to predict talented performance. Being a member of MENSA requires an IQ above 132, but what has MENSA ever done of note?

The point? Some people may be naturally better equipped to excel in certain areas or fields than others, yes. But as the Gallup research shows—and this may strike some as a statement of faith and optimism—all humans are blessed with certain skills and abilities. They are not all identical, and some might be less inclined than others to pursue, say, marine biology or graphic design, but we all have value that can translate and be lent toward the greater good of ourselves and our communities.

So what America needs is not more virtuosos with one-in-a-million, once-in-a-lifetime abilities in some chosen field. Not at all. The endless stories about the mind-boggling financial successes of tech industry leaders like Bill Gates and Mark Zuckerberg may leave the mistaken impression that innate ability combined with an incredible drive is enough. But it's not. College dropouts who go on to become corporate titans are fascinating but wholly unlikely scenarios. Planning to take that route is a bit like ditching your plans to invest in a 401(k) and buying lottery tickets instead. The fact is that higher education is all but required for entry into the executive suite. According to surveys by executive search firm Spencer Stuart, 97 percent of CEOs at Fortune 500 companies have a four-year college degree, and 62 percent have advanced degrees.[50]

This doesn't just apply to CEOs. It applies to all workers. And certain aspects of talent are clearly more important than others. In earlier economies, success at work depended largely on muscle—for those who tilled the soil—as well as some understanding of machinery; for factory workers, success involved those things as well as manual dexterity and a knack for teamwork. Workers today, and for tomorrow, need a deeper and broader set of skills, knowledge, and abilities. Basic computer competence, to cite just one example, is now a necessity for everyone from hedge fund managers to factory workers.

Figure 1. The Percentage of Occupations Requiring Average Levels of Mental KSAs Increased Over Time

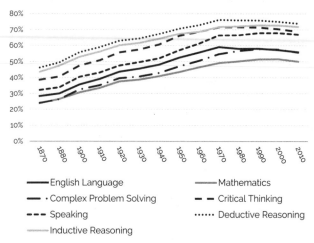

Source: Georgetown University Center on Education and the Workforce analysis of O*NET 18.0 and IPUMS (1870–2010)

Figure 2. The Percentage of Occupations Requiring Average Levels of Physical KSAs Decreased Over Time

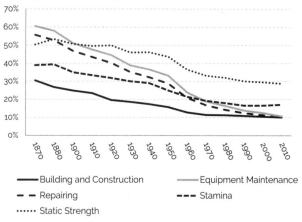

Source: Georgetown University Center on Education and the Workforce analysis of O*NET 18.0 and IPUMS (1870–2010)

Knowledge ranges from a general understanding of basic math, science, and humanities, to specific knowledge in more applied disciplines, such as accounting or engineering. Knowledge in one occupation has always been transferable to others. What you learn from being a salesperson can give you a leg up on starting a consumer-oriented business because you understand customers. But the evolving ways in which knowledge is being produced and used are ushering in more interdisciplinary academic and hybrid-career programs. Preparing for these careers will require a mix of job-specific technical preparation and a foundation in other disciplines.

At the same time, that growth in overlapping assignments and performance goals increases the need for cross-training and soft skills like communications and teamwork. Think about the analogy to fitness. We've moved from a model where calisthenics—repetitive, tightly controlled exercise of specific muscle groups—has been replaced by the more modern approach of cross-training, where different muscle groups are used in different combinations, resulting in a greater level of overall fitness. As technology automates repetitive tasks in every occupation, for example, workers are left to perform more general, nonrepetitive functions like quality control and innovation. These require more interaction with other workers across disciplines and occupations.

Skills are basically the ability to acquire and impart knowledge. Content skills include speaking and writing; processing skills include critical thinking; and problem-solving skills involve identifying complex problems in order to arrive at solutions and implement them. The skills needed for one job may be transferable to another even when specific knowledge is not: Good "people" skills, for instance, are equally useful to a teacher or a CEO. But the skills a worker brings to a job do not always match the job. A skill mismatch could mean a worker is overskilled, which is a waste of resources, or underskilled, which could mean less effective or less productive. Of the two problems, underskilled workers cause the greatest concern for employers, educators, and policy makers.

Analytical, managerial, and social skills are the skills that are most valued by the workers themselves. Analytical skills—by which I mean critical thinking and complex problem solving—are "very important" to 25 percent of workers and "important" to 65 percent. Mathematical/technical, resource management, and mechanical skills are less valued by workers, with 20 percent or more ranking them as "not important." This makes sense: Analytical, management, and social skills are applicable to almost every occupation, while those other skills are usually more job-specific.

Figure 3. Importance of Knowledge Factors Throughout the Economy - 2011

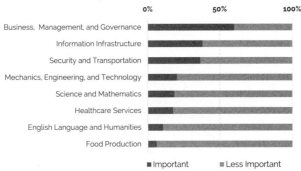

Source: Georgetown University Center on Education and the Workforce analysis of O*NET 17.0 and ACS 2011

Figure 4. Importance of Skills Factors Throughout the Economy - 2011

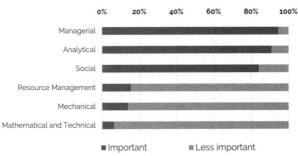

Source: Georgetown University Center on Education and the Workforce analysis of O*NET 17.0 and ACS 2011

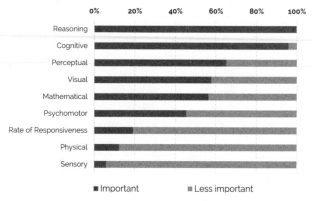

Figure 5. Importance of Ability Factors Throughout the Economy - 2011

Source: Georgetown University Center on Education and the Workforce analysis of O*NET 17.0 and ACS 2011

Abilities are personal attributes and aptitudes that influence work performance. These include things like an aptitude for mathematical reasoning or a talent for oral and written expression. Abilities, like skills, are associated with the capacity to apply knowledge to solve problems. However, abilities are generally believed to be much more stable and enduring than skills. Skills can be learned; abilities are to some extent present in a person at an early age and developed over time. They include generic characteristics that allow individuals to acquire a skill.

In general, workers value thinking more than doing in our economy. Cognitive and reasoning abilities top the list of valued abilities, followed closely by perceptual, visual, and mathematical abilities. Psychomotor, physical, and rate of responsiveness are ranked in descending order of importance; the last is sensory abilities, which more than 60 percent of workers ranked as "not important."

My view is that we all have talent, we all have promise, and we all have potential to put it to use. Some will create and invent, others will educate, some will head large corporations, others will start small businesses, some will study the stars, and others will till the land.

It's in there, in everyone. In so many cases, we just need to find a way to bring it forward. Importantly, this match is most often hampered by socioeconomic status.

Lots of less-advantaged Americans never get the chance to fully develop their talents. The seminal work of Eric Turkheimer and his team at the University of Virginia shows that, for most low-income kids, there is no relationship between innate abilities measured in childhood and aptitudes developed by the time they are old enough for college.[51] In other words, if you come from a poor or working-poor family, chances are you won't ever get the opportunity to "be all you can be."

For the most part, kids who come from families that make more than $60,000 a year do get a shot at being all they can be. Income trumps innate ability as a predictor of college access among working-poor families. Conversely, innate ability trumps income among middle-class and upper-class kids. Most of the difference in the developed aptitudes among college-age middle- and upper-income adolescents can be accounted for by measured differences in their innate abilities when they were children.

For many young people, the odds of getting out from under this structural bias and on to college are not good. Sociologists Tim Smeeding and Lee Rainwater made this point two decades ago in a seminal report that showed the United States to be the breakaway leader in an international competition we don't want to win: the share of children living in poverty. In a peer group of affluent countries, even after government help is figured in, the US ranked poorly.[52] Not much has changed in the ensuing years. A 2013 report from UNICEF comparing twenty-nine developed countries shows that the US ranks twenty-sixth in the overall well-being of children, with only Lithuania, Latvia, and Romania trailing the US in this depressing race to the bottom.[53]

Nancy Zimpher, chancellor of the 450,000-student State University of New York system, has also taught and administered at Ohio State and the University of Wisconsin–Milwaukee, and was president of the University of Cincinnati. In each of these contexts, she gathered quite a bit of insight into talent and how it develops.

"Talent evolves from giving people opportunity," she says. "If young people, as well as adults, are provided access to ideas, allowed to be creative, to be literate both in language and calculation, the rest will take care of itself."

But the rest can't take care of itself if those opportunities are not available. "Talent comes from opportunity, and what this country is tipping towards is less opportunity," Zimpher observes, with dismay. "And with a massive new population evolving, we need access to opportunity now more than ever."

The problem we are facing isn't that Americans don't have the inherent abilities. It's that these abilities are not being cultivated fast enough. For the synergistic potential of talent to rise in every human, we need to have the mechanisms in place for it to find daylight. Millions of Americans possess talent and a set of interests that they may not even be aware of. All too often, as in the case of many first-generation and minority Americans, the opportunities just don't exist for that talent to ever surface.

Broken cities and failing schools that extinguish the flicker of talent from an early age, a higher education system that does far too little to guide students lucky enough to get onto campus to areas that touch on their strengths, and a bewilderingly dysfunctional immigration system (because there is plenty of talent abroad waiting to be cultivated as well) are all part of the problem. All part of the talent block.

What follows is a framework for how we remove that block and a formula for how to isolate, incubate, and unleash the talent that I believe exists in all Americans in some form. The Five Ways to attract, educate, and deploy talent represent the best opportunities to move the needle on America's talent challenge. When this happens, when our interests and our passions are matched to our abilities and credentials, we will prosper as human beings and, as a result, as a society.

PART II

FIVE WAYS TO ATTRACT, EDUCATE, AND DEPLOY TALENT

5

IT'S THE LEARNING, STUPID

Have you heard about the graduate from Stanford who went deeply in debt getting a degree in classics, only to find no job on the other side of graduation? Now she's prepping iced caramel macchiatos for minimum wage.

How about the philosophy major from Michigan who's paying off his student loans by stocking shelves at Target while living at home with his parents?

Let's not forget the art history student who studied Michelangelo at Johns Hopkins and ended up flipping burgers at McDonald's.

And have you read all the alarming headlines?

"College Is Dead," declared *Time*.[54] "For Most People, College Is a Waste of Time," says *The Wall Street Journal*.[55] The same publication also asks, "Do Too Many Young People Go to College?"[56]

Elsewhere, The Huffington Post tells us "Why College Is Usually a Waste of Time,"[57] while Rush Limbaugh decries the "Big Education Racket."[58]

Scan the blogs and you will see headlines like "College Is a Waste of Time." Or "College Is a Ludicrous Waste of Money." Or the slightly more multi-faceted "College Is a Waste of Time and Money," and also "College Is a HUGE Waste of Time." Thanks for the clarification.

PayPal cofounder Peter Thiel created a fellowship in 2012 to encourage Americans under the age of twenty to *drop out* of college and pursue entrepreneurial work. He's paying for 100 of them to do so. He hasn't yet explained how the other nineteen million students who currently go to college can find their own Uncle Peter.[59]

Thus we find what is certainly one of the most prevalent media memes of the past few years: Go to college and you will end up studying some useless field, get a degree that has zero applicable use in getting a job, go deeply in debt to do so, and go straight from commencement to waiting tables, tending bar, or sweeping floors while living in the bedroom you grew up in. Who on earth would sign up for and spend their money on that? So, the argument goes, fewer and fewer people should pursue higher education.

As far back as the 1970s, there was talk of "over-educated Americans" and dead-end educational opportunities.[60] Newspapers were printing stories about college graduates who were scraping by at menial jobs that had no earthly relation to the rarefied field of study they pursued in college. The imminent demise of higher education is not a new theory. Nor is the argument that getting a postsecondary degree is futile. This is what I like to call a zombie doctrine. No matter how many times you try to slay it, it comes back to life, stronger each time.

But if we are to grow America's talent, we will have to slay the undead once and for all.

As discussed, before the 1950s, the college degree was a rare commodity. But in the wake of the GI Bill, it went from being an accoutrement of the elite to the nationally acknowledged credential showing you are qualified for success in the job market. And no matter how many scary scenarios the mainstream media presents about the sad fate of college grads and the uselessness of their degrees, it still is the key to employment.

Let's not kid ourselves: America's higher education system is indeed in need of an overhaul. But let's draw a distinction between murdering higher education and modernizing it. The former will cause us to slip behind in the talent contest. The latter is our first key to winning it.

Here is a quick rundown of what must change:

- College must become more affordable and accessible.

- Prices must be more transparent.

- Education must foster more creativity and risk-taking to help solve the nation's entrenched social and economic problems.

- Federal and state governments must coordinate education policies with institutions of higher learning.

- And those schools need to catch up to and take advantage of current technologies.

Big data, online programs, and the explosion of social media have transformed teaching and forced huge changes in every corner of the higher education system, from assessment and accreditation, to student recruitment and support, to faculty hiring and development. Each is part of the overall redesign of higher education already under way.

There is no shortage of ideas about how to redesign higher education, some better than others. Take Massive Open Online Courses, or MOOCs, for example. No innovation in higher education has received more attention from the national media than MOOCs. This may be in part because the biggest names in the world of MOOCs—Coursera, EdX, Udacity—have their origins in universities with global reputations, including Stanford, Harvard, and MIT.

MOOCs are an interesting point on the continuum of non-classroom-based learning in higher education. Starting in the 1960s, "distance education" consisted of correspondence courses that offered independent study via the mail. Students would receive course materials, take exams, and be graded by a professor (usually one hired by a for-profit company that was offering the correspondence course), all for a fixed fee. Few correspondence courses were available where students could receive actual credits from an accredited college or university.

In the 1980s, technology took the idea of distance learning a step further. Satellite technology, videotapes, and other media were used to transmit information to students faster than the older mail-based correspondence courses. The advent of the global Internet in the 1990s continued this advancement, giving learners access to materials and courses that were previously available only through classroom-based settings. Some of these became connected to the regular curriculums of colleges and universities, allowing students to receive course credits.

In each of these cases, the material being transmitted was essentially the same as or similar to what was provided in classrooms. MOOCs are an extension of that model, with the added notion that there could be unlimited numbers of students participating—tens of thousands in some cases. It's likely that the scale potential of MOOCs, combined with the reputations of the institutions and people behind their creation, was at least partially responsible for the near-hysteria about MOOCs that emerged in 2012 and 2013.

Yet the current limitation of MOOCs is fairly obvious. Even with the added value of being able to access video clips, problem sets, and other information beyond traditional course materials, MOOCs are largely still a transmission model, simply an extension of the model that has existed for decades.

Much has been written about the dramatic drop-off in interest in MOOCs from prospective learners—the thousands that sign up in the beginning rapidly dwindle to hundreds once the course assignments and more serious work begins. Colleges themselves also have waning interest. A survey of more than 3,000 academic leaders in 2014 showed a dramatic decline in the development of new MOOCs compared to 2012, when the craze really began. The *Chronicle of Higher Education* headline says it all: "The MOOC Hype Fades."[61]

Over the longer term, MOOCs may very well have a place in the ecosystem of learning, a sort of extension of the role of traditional colleges and universities. More interesting, though, is the ways in which technology is being used not as a transmission tool, but as an interactive learning platform, where the technology adapts to and targets the lessons based on what students already have learned. The best example of this may be the Open Learning Initiative established by Carnegie Mellon University. OLI, as it is called, began in the early 2000s and has been widely tested in a variety of course contexts, ranging from English and French to chemistry and statistics. OLI essentially redesigns general education courses (using highly advanced learning science techniques) so that they can be completed faster—sometimes twice as fast—as traditional courses. The kicker is that student performance and knowledge retention often is the same or better over time as it is in traditional classrooms.[62]

Many of the different approaches to redesigning higher education like OLI have value. But on their own they are unlikely to change the system overall. In part, this is because the idea of a "system" of higher education may be one of the most difficult concepts to alter in our psyche. For much of the past century and a half, the "system" consisted of different combinations of colleges and universities—elite and open-access; research-oriented, teaching-focused; and community colleges, public and private. All of these different combinations led us to the not-unreasonable conclusion that our system of higher education was the most diverse in nature, most inclusive in its admissions, and the "best" based on the international reputational ranking of our top research universities.

Yet the "system" has already begun to evolve. Many commentators, including Clay Christensen and Thomas Friedman, have argued that the industry of higher education is ripe for disruption, and that there's a revolution already underway in that industry. To paraphrase the seventies jazz poet Gil Scott-Heron, the revolution is being televised, blogged, tweeted, and MOOC'ed in ways that we could never even have dreamed just a few years ago. And it's dramatically changing what people learn, where they learn it, and how they will use it in work and in life. As a result, we see evidence that "the system" is really an ecosystem of people, with students at the center: Institutions of higher education, with faculty playing an especially important role; policy and professional organizations; employers; and others are other major elements of that system. In other words, the colleges and universities aren't the system, and the fact that we still see it that way confuses and perhaps even confounds progress at a time when the urgency for change is high.

Now, this doesn't mean that colleges and universities as we know them are suddenly superfluous. Far from it. The knowledge-development role that colleges and universities play is critical, as is their broader role of service to community and society. But the institutional focus of the system—the idea that decisions and funding and policies should primarily respond to the needs of colleges and universities—is no longer appropriate, if it ever was. It must be replaced by a focus on meeting the needs of students and, by extension, the needs of society.

A redesign of college must also recognize that students themselves have changed. The traditional picture of a college student—eighteen years old, fresh out of high school, headed to campus for the first time, and destined to work the same job or career from graduation until retirement—is as antiquated as the system they are about to be submerged in. In fact, if you count the students who go to college with the support of their parents, attend full-time, and live in college housing, you end up describing less than one out of every four college students today.[63]

Today's student population is huge and growing and remarkably diverse; in fact, it looks nothing like your father's freshman class or even your own freshman classes. (I went to college in the eighties, and have the skinny ties and R.E.M. albums to prove it.) The 21st century student represents all ages and income groups, all races and ethnicities, part-time and full-time students, living on and way off campus, pursuing not just four-year degrees but also adding skills and credentials of all kinds to their personal portfolios. The main thing they all have in common is a search for a better and bigger return on their investment.

And college, for that matter, no longer looks like the college we still see in movies or television: It's not ivy-covered towers, professors in tweed, and students packed into lecture halls or poring over books in dorms. It's students studying at community colleges—who alone represent almost one-half of the enrollment in US higher education—to adult learners taking undergraduate and graduate classes from for-profit entities. It's online, on iPads, at a distance, at dinner tables, and in videoconference rooms.

Indeed, it's becoming increasingly clear that "college-level learning" does not even need to take place in a traditional institution of higher education as we know it. With the emergence of trends like taking a person's prior military, education, national service, or work experience and assigning actual credit or value to it in a college context—prior learning assessment— we see the emergence of a new paradigm. In this new world, providing students smarter pathways into and through higher education will be critical. All learning should count; everyone should know what degrees represent so they can be put to use most effectively, whether it's for employment or further education; and everyone should know the next step they need to take to move toward their personal goals.

At its root, we need to rethink and reimagine the entire premise of higher education. We must ask ourselves what type of product we want to be sold and produced by the nation's colleges and universities and other providers of postsecondary learning.

To me, one answer is a system that cultivates and tracks talent, and deploys a prepared and imaginative workforce that can obtain and create jobs, becomes this century's bold innovators, and ensures that America thrives in the global economy. It's a system that produces people who lead a good, moral, globally literate, and civically engaged and responsible life that we can all share. Higher education must be redesigned so that it truly serves our needs as a society.

One of the best commentators and critics of the current model of American higher education, Kevin Carey, eloquently describes this path to higher education transformation in his 2015 book, *The End of College*. I count Kevin as a friend and ferociously smart colleague, and have learned a great deal from his insights on a variety of topics, college-level learning outcomes, student financing, and new postsecondary education delivery models, to name just a few. And his observation about getting to a true system redesign, I think, perfectly summarizes what's ahead. "Many of those who have lived and learned in colleges as we know them cherish their memory and institutions," Carey writes, "But the way we know them is not the only way they can be. Our lifetimes will see the birth of a better, higher learning."[64]

He's right. And the single most drastic, effective, and yes, revolutionary, way to get there has to do with the end of time as we know it.

Perhaps the most outdated feature of our current higher education system is how we measure learning. Today, this is done according to the amount of time spent at desks and in classrooms—or sometimes even time spent online—rather than by how much students actually absorb and subsequently what they do with that knowledge.

But what would happen if we turned this system on its head? What if college credits were awarded based not on seat time, but rather on measurable learning? What if we prioritized outcomes over inputs?

Dating from the early days of the 20th century, the standard unit of college currency has been the credit hour. This, like so many of our institutions, came about by accident. At the beginning of the 20th century, when Andrew Carnegie attempted to adjust the low pay of professors at Cornell University, on whose board he served as a trustee, he created a pension system, which was then offered to other universities with a catch: All schools that bought into the pension plan, now known as TIAA-CREF, had to adopt the credit-hour system, which the National Education Association had used to determine high school credit.[65] And with that, the Carnegie Unit became the standard metric of a student's fluency in a subject, both in college and high school. Today, 120 hours usually equals a bachelor's degree.

And yet the credit hour was never meant to measure how much a student *actually* learned. The colleges and universities are merely measuring how many hours students put in, not what they are truly getting out of it or what they will take with them into the job market. To make matters worse, this outdated metric is totally unsuited to measuring many of the innovations that have the potential to reshape higher education. Online learning and curriculum customized to a student's needs and ambitions, for example, don't mesh with a system that relies solely on hours logged to determine what is being learned. And the credit hour isn't even really "currency": Many institutions don't even accept credit transfers, or do so with so many caveats that no one who doesn't already have a degree can figure out how it works. It's a currency that all too often has no exchange rate.

So it's *time* for a change. It's time for a system that awards learning credits that are based on *learning*, not time. It's time for a student-centered credentialing system that prioritizes what you know and can do over where and how you get your education. And the only way to do this is to remove and replace the credit hour.

How do we do this? Obviously, there are a lot of parts to this puzzle. Still, we know the basic aspects of the higher education system the nation needs: At its core, it's a system that offers multiple, clearly marked pathways to various levels of student success—pathways that are affordable, clear, and interconnected, with no dead ends, no cul-de-sacs, and plenty of on- and off-ramps.

Second, these pathways must be built on the foundation of learning, with degrees and other postsecondary credentials representing those well-defined and transparent results mentioned a moment ago, validated through quality assessment. And as I noted earlier, all learning certified as high quality should count—no matter how, when, or where it was obtained.

In the ideal scenario, then, in this new system every student will know where he or she is going, how much it will cost to get there, how much time it will take, and what to expect at journey's end—both in terms of learning outcomes and career prospects.

We don't have the luxury of commissioning long studies on how to make such a system a reality. Time really is our enemy at this point, given the urgency of our national need for talent. We also know that change is never easy. Still, the payoff for making this change will be huge, so let's explore how it can happen.

Two major shifts in thinking need to undergird the system-redesign project, a pair of new perspectives that must drive all of the smaller changes. One has to do with how we might envision a system where institutions of higher education are no longer at the center. The other has to do with how the shift from a time-based system to a learning-focused one will actually happen.

In place of the time-based method of "keeping score," a system must be constructed that defines, fosters, measures, and rewards what truly matters: student learning.

I don't think I can overstate this point when it comes to the redesigned higher education system: We must focus on learning outcomes as the true measure of educational quality. Not time, not institutional reputation (like the *US News & World Report* and other rankings do), but genuine learning: that is, those competencies that are informed by the real world in which students must thrive.

This will not be easy. Traditionally, Americans have highly correlated where they went to school with who they are. Take a look at the Facebook accounts of anyone who has been to college. Most people list the school they attended as a key part of who they are—right alongside other important life information like relationship status, hometown, and current job.

More important, until fairly recently, employers often associated where people went to college with the quality of education they received. But as a recent survey of employers showed, employers are no longer on board with this outdated idea: Only 14 percent believe colleges and universities are preparing students adequately for work.[66] Indeed, another survey of college alumni conducted by Gallup and Purdue University found that the factors associated with having a great job and a great life—workplace engagement and personal well-being—have no correlation with where you went to school. None. Ivy League versus public university, Top 100 rated versus others. It didn't matter.[67]

The proxy measures for quality have been just that—proxies. But as a better understanding of what higher education produces for society has developed—what we need it to produce in terms of more talent and better talented citizens—it's become clear that these proxies are insufficient.

Think about the analogy to healthcare. We have more and better information than ever before about patients. Detailed data on their prior health status, combined with carefully understood and controlled treatments, have given us a much-improved understanding of whether someone is healthy or not. Objective indicators from blood tests and the like, combined with qualitative judgments of the professionals treating the patients, give us very good information to assess patient progress, determine further treatment options, and ultimately conclude whether or how they can function going forward.

In healthcare, these objective measures are generally accepted and understood. But in education, and especially higher education, it's hard to know how well someone is doing. We don't have a common basis for understanding what degrees or other credentials represent in terms of learning. We simply use the accumulation of credits as a proxy—120 credit hours for a bachelor's degree, sixty for an associate, etc. And we don't have a clear enough understanding of which methods (like instructional pedagogies, counseling strategies, academic support interventions, or financing mechanisms) actually matter. So we use the mother of all proxies, "reputation," as a substitute for that understanding. You went to Harvard (or Williams, or Stanford, or UT-Austin)? OK, then that must mean you're smart and capable of doing great things, just because you attended and accumulated enough of those time-based units of progress called credits at a certain school. To extend the healthcare analogy, it's a bit like saying, "Hey, she was a patient at the Cleveland Clinic, spent five days there, and was discharged, so she must be healthy." Really?

The shift to a student-centered, learning-based approach to postsecondary learning is the key. It is the foundation for that overarching, fully linked system of education that runs from pre-K, through higher education, into the workforce, and even beyond.

What's happening is really a shift in the mode of learning that is quite fundamental. Learning has historically been seen as a linear activity—you start with elementary school, middle school, and high school, and then continue on to postsecondary education—a community college, four-year school, graduate, or professional school.

Much the same is true for work. Historically, people tended to work in the same company, or at least the same industry, for their entire career, working their way up a linear ladder.

Now, however, we see the nature of work changing in profound ways. According to the federal Bureau of Labor Statistics—the people who track unemployment, among other things—people not only change jobs more frequently than in the past, they also change industries, often multiple times. In 2013, *Failure to Launch*, a look at the dynamics of the 21st-century job market released by the Georgetown University's Center on Education and the Workforce, reported that "Young people today change jobs more frequently... and only one out of 10 describes his or her current job as a career." The numbers reveal the shift: "The average worker in the millennial generation changes jobs 6.3 times between the ages of 18 and 25, compared to 5.5 times for the average baby boomer when he or she was between 18 and 25.9."[68]

Talent, I've noted, is cumulative—what you've learned and applied from that learning in the past gets added to what you learn and do now. But what's changing is that both learning and work are moving away from this linear model to something much more like the now-overused term of "cloud computing." People now have access to learning opportunities and jobs that are not linear in nature. You can acquire high-quality learning in many different unbundled ways—in traditional classroom-based learning, online from numerous different sources, and from work and personal experiences. All of these things, combined, add to the talent you have as an individual.

So the linear, time-based methods of assessing or assigning "credit" for learning are clearly going to need to change. Higher education analyst and reformer Amy Laitinen made the case for "cracking the credit hour" in a 2012 report that laid out the pathway to a new time-less system of higher education.[69] As good as this intelligently written, contemporary report is, this 1938 quote that Laitinen uncovered from Carnegie Foundation president Walter Jessup sums up the point as well as if it were being said today:

> [T]he system of units and credits, which, useful as it was a third of a century ago, is not good enough for American education today. …American higher education appears to be well on its way to another stage of development in which promotion, at least in college, will be based upon 'the attainments of minds thoroughly stored and competent.'

Great. So now we are finally getting around to shifting the system toward learning and student outcomes and away from institutions and time-based units of measurement. How do we do that? And more important, how do we actually accelerate that process to better meet our rapidly emerging needs as a nation?

An entire set of books needs to be written on this subject alone, but let me offer a few basic ideas.

First, we need to stop assuming that the way we've always done it is the best way, or the only way. Remember, our chief enemy in this process is time. So what if we sped up the learning process, not by pushing people to unreasonable levels, but by making it clear that they've got to stay on task and demonstrate that they've learned something, and then getting them into the labor market faster? How do we develop and implement systems of learning that follow the maxim of legendary basketball coach John Wooden: "Be quick, but don't hurry"?

The answer is that we need scalable, high-quality, low-cost accelerated postsecondary education programs. One illustration of this approach is Ivy Tech Community College of Indiana, which rolled out its Associate Accelerated Program (ASAP) in 2010. The program identifies potential students while they are still in high school, most from families living below the poverty line, and offers the opportunity to earn an outcomes-oriented associate degree—one that's both marketable and transferable—in just twelve months. In this program, students are block-scheduled from 9 to 2 or 9 to 4 each day, and are provided various support services, thereby allowing them to treat the program like a full-time job, attending class with their cohort forty hours per week. The results have been highly encouraging—really, they've exceeded expectations. According to Ivy Tech, after twelve months in the program, 86 percent of ASAP students earned a degree or are still enrolled—a rate five times as good as the average Ivy Tech student.[70]

Speed, however, is not enough. Competency, deep proficiency, is critical to success in the workplace, and in life. It makes little sense to learn things that don't matter, and it makes even less sense to study but not learn anything. Here's where the rapidly emerging movement toward competency-based learning is critical.

Competency-based education (or CBE in the jargon of educators) is, in a nutshell, education designed around the mastery of a defined set of skills. Of course, mastery is the objective of all educational programs. However, CBE is based on defining the expected educational outcomes of a program of study as a set of skills (competencies) along with criteria for demonstrating mastery of them. In CBE, the program of study is designed around the orderly and sequential mastery of the competencies. Naturally, CBE has been used in higher education for many years and is the standard model of learning in many fields of study, particularly for occupational skills. What is changing is the idea that CBE could be used much more widely in higher education, both to reach larger numbers of students—particularly adult learners—and in fields of study beyond the occupational areas in which CBE has traditionally been applied.

Now, however, we see a relative explosion in competency-based learning models. The approaches being pioneered nationally by Western Governors University, Brandman University, and the University of Wisconsin system, to name just a few, have taken advantage of the transformative power of technology to develop rigorous, demanding, and learning-focused programs of study unlike what we've seen before. I believe these models will be scaling quickly, and represent a sea change in the way in which postsecondary learning is delivered.

Martha Kanter, who served as undersecretary of Education during the Obama administration, has been an advocate of competency-based learning. She sees this emerging approach as a key element of the system redesign necessary in the higher education realm.

"How do you unleash talent in untraditional ways so students can realize their full potential?" Kanter asked me during a conversation about education and talent development. "It's going to be through crowd-sourcing the diversity of human experience towards higher and higher levels of competence. And that will ultimately help students both learn and grow."

This idea of crowdsourcing learning is at the root of the competency-based movement. It acknowledges that *where* students learn is not nearly as important as *what* they know and can *do*, and that the learning itself can take place in many different contexts, from a plethora of different sources and learning materials. Anytime. Anyplace. Anywhere.

One of the most impressive emerging models of CBE is an entity that has sprung up in the heart of traditional higher education—New England. It's called College for America (CfA), an offshoot of Southern New Hampshire University.

CfA is the first of its kind: an accredited competency-based college program, completely unmoored to the Carnegie Unit. The platform, which offers students a total of 120 different competencies, has no actual courses, no classrooms, and no professors. Instead of measuring by hours, students earn credit, so to speak, and then degrees, by showing mastery of their chosen competency.

A year's worth of work on a degree cost $2,500 in 2014. So, two years of work will cost $5,000, but those who can finish in less than a year can get a degree for as low as $1,250.[71] Paul J. LeBlanc, the president of Southern New Hampshire University, describes CfA's goals with his usual blunt effectiveness: "Let time be variable, but make learning well-defined, fixed and non-negotiable."[72] They are one of the first to institutionalize this model, but certainly not the last.

Despite the promise of CfA and its affordable degrees, a question remains: How will we pay for learning in this time-less, learning-outcomes-driven system of postsecondary education? This problem has vexed analysts for the past several years as competency-based learning models have proliferated. For places like CfA, which was established as a separate unit of an existing institution, there are some built-in benefits. Start-up costs are fewer, and the school can take advantage of existing resources like the teaching faculty to design and deliver the curriculum. On the other hand, the costs of developing the curriculums, assessment systems, and back-office supports (for things like course registration and grading) might be extensive, especially since many of the existing systems are based on a credit model and not transferable to this new approach.[73]

Student costs are the other part of the equation. A flat "all you can eat" pricing model is fairly clean from the student/consumer perspective. But does it work? The US Department of Education made an important decision in 2013 to permit some experimentation with competency-based learning for the purposes of eligibility for federal student aid programs. These are important experiments, conducted by willing participants from across the spectrum of colleges and universities. They will provide much-needed information about how these models may impact the broader effort to shift the system away from institutions and time and toward students and learning. They may also reveal whether there are differences for public versus private schools, or for students studying to get associate versus bachelor's degrees.

One radical model, though still realistic, would be to shift government support toward a single pot of resources that every person would be eligible to draw from, sort of like a line of credit or a personal trust fund. Each person would be allocated a fixed dollar amount of funds to draw from in support of postsecondary learning. They could use those funds to pay for learning at a number of different, approved learning providers that have demonstrated results that align with specific competencies or proficiencies.

In this model, the resources are the purview of the individual, not the provider. In other words, it is student-managed, and student-driven.

This idea, which might be called the Talent Trust, harkens back to proposals that have been made in the past for things like government-sponsored savings plans and government-supported trust funds, like Social Security for education. One proposal that I played a role in was called the Student's Total Education Package, or STEP, developed under the auspices of the bipartisan federal commission mentioned earlier that was tasked with developing big new ideas to help make college more affordable.[74]

STEP essentially was a proposal to set the amount of total federal assistance that goes to students to support their undergraduate educations—at the time it was written in 1993, that amount was $14,000. This fixed sum would not be allocated to all students in the same way, however. STEP proposed that existing grant, loan, and other programs be harmonized in a way that resulted in a sliding subsidy scale, where the students with the greatest financial need (usually the lowest income) would receive all or most of the aid in the form of grants, while those in the middle would receive a mix, and those at the high end would receive essentially a subsidy that amounted to a guarantee against default, but little other support in terms of interest rate relief.

Though many of the other National Commission's recommendations dealing with tax policy and the student loan delivery system were implemented, STEP never took off. One reason was practical: Getting from the existing array of federal grant, loan, work-study, and other programs to this system of a sliding subsidy scale made the heads of the legislative drafters hurt.

But STEP, or at least elements of it, may just have been a solution not quite ripe for the problems it intended to solve. It was a student-focused model proposed at a time when institutions were the main thing policy makers could relate to when thinking about improving the system. The not-too-distant future will require a financing system in which students can gain access to resources that pay for the outcomes, not the time spent. It also will need to make sure that students can use financial support to pay for different modes of delivery at a multitude of providers: Some may be in a classroom where credits are still the coin of the realm, some may be in competency-based learning contexts, and some might be in entities like libraries, unions, community-based organizations, companies, and other entities that have been certified to provide specific types of learning.

What's different about the Talent Trust is that it puts the decision-making for how to allocate those resources in the hands of the learner. The learner would be able to decide the best path that meets both her learning objectives and financial circumstances. This creates a much freer market for learners to participate in deciding the end game, rather than placing sole responsibility in the hands of the providers.

Getting from here to there will no doubt be a challenge. There will be winners and losers in this type of system, and some will seek to game it. But if learning outcomes are at the core of what we expect in our talent development system, such a financing strategy would represent a way of making sure that the funds actually flow in the direction of achieving those outcomes, and not toward merely achieving the desired outcomes of the institutions or other providers.

Not so long ago, the inescapable catchphrase in public and political discourse was "It's the economy, stupid." The phrase remains accurate, in many ways. Economic concerns still trump most others, and that's unlikely to ever change. But that message, coined in the early nineties by political strategist James Carville, is a bit imprecise these days. Today, as the pundits and politicians constantly remind us, it's not simply about the economy. Specifically, it's about talent— or the lack thereof. Focusing our higher education system on learning, which is how we get to the higher levels of talent, is a sure way to meet the nation's economic success.

Maybe the catchphrase of the future needs to be "It's the learning, stupid," because learning is the key to system redesign. Changing how we pay for the outcomes we want and need from our postsecondary learning system, and not the time people spend, is critical to this redesigned system, which in turn is essential to the development of talent in the United States. Government plays a big role in this, because it is so dominant in the student financing equation. And so do the postsecondary providers themselves— no longer just colleges and universities, but a whole panoply of places and participants.

Doesn't the private sector have an important role to play as well? Let's look at that next.

6

UNLEASHING PRIVATE SECTOR INNOVATION

A more talented nation won't happen on its own. Lots of different people and institutions will need to be involved. Government has a role, of course, because it has the capacity to deliver at scale in ways that others cannot. But let's be clear: This is not government's problem to solve on its own. Philanthropic organizations, employers, capital markets, and other private sector institutions all have important roles to play.

Greater talent has implications for our collective well-being, and that means all of the important players need to do their part. Private philanthropy certainly is one key. The foundation that I am privileged to lead, Lumina Foundation, is one of more than 80,000 private foundations in the United States, with combined assets in excess of $600 billion as of 2013. With the amount of financial resources we have and the expertise we have developed by being so deeply involved in the work, foundations like Lumina have leadership responsibility. Making grants to support nonprofits is necessary but not sufficient.

It's not that charity doesn't matter. Quite the contrary: The charitable impulse—that mysterious, marvelous urge to give, to help, to meet the needs of others—is fundamental to our humanity. Without it, true opportunity is unattainable. Charity still matters a great deal.

But it's not enough—and charity is not philanthropy.

At its core, charity is about help, about meeting urgent needs. Philanthropy, though, is about change. Philanthropy is focused not on symptoms, but on root causes. It is systemic, not episodic; proactive rather than reactive. In short, the goal of philanthropy is not so much to provide assistance or service; rather, it seeks to permanently alter the conditions that make assistance necessary.

What this means is that, in order to effect significant and lasting change, a philanthropic organization must be a leadership organization, both in thought and in action. It must set an agenda for change, and then work purposefully and consistently to produce results.

Philanthropy has one important role to play in helping the nation get to a higher level of talent. Foundations can take the risks that others cannot—pushing for the most promising ideas, and helping take them to scale. Philanthropy's risk tolerance is often higher than that of many of the other key players. We won't get voted out of office for taking risk, the way policy makers might, nor do we face incurring the wrath of restless shareholders, the way a publicly traded company might.

Another key private sector player that needs to be tapped in the talent drive is private capital markets. Think about it. Compared to the $622 billion in US foundation assets, global capital markets represent $212 trillion in "tappable" resources. If one one-hundredth of a percent of those resources were applied to addressing the talent deficit in the United States, we'd suddenly have more than $200 billion in additional resources that could be put to work. Several private foundations have been wrestling with how to access just a tiny fraction of those funds to generate potentially huge social impact. A new social economy—including foundations, nonprofits, and new types of enterprises created to support public benefit—is emerging to engage these larger capital markets.

"There are those in the private market who think that government should occupy this space," observes Mohamed El-Erian. "Then there are those who say we need to be involved, because it's the right thing to do. And then there are those who truly believe they can change things."

Employers of all types also have a central role that relates to what El-Erian says. Indeed, we can point to the likes of Michael Bloomberg, Eli Broad, and Marissa Mayer as shining examples of the last group—the changers. But there are arguably not enough of these difference-makers, and not enough examples of private-public collaboration. "This is really unfortunate," says El-Erian. "These partnerships allow for better burden sharing. The government has the ability to coordinate and overcome market failures; the private sector brings the expertise and money."

So what can philanthropy, employers, and private capital markets do in concert to help make the nation more talented? One approach might be to expand our notion of where talent gets cultivated, and who should actually be recognized as providers of talent development. It's long been understood that formal schooling, both in public and private settings, is part of our national talent growth efforts. More recently, we've seen an increasing interest within private companies, like Starbucks, taking more direct responsibility for the education of their employees—even if some of those educated at the employer's expense don't actually end up staying at that employer after they've achieved higher skill levels.

"There is a heart and a history in this company. We care about our people and want to invest in them," observes Blair Taylor, Starbucks' chief community officer (CCO). "But we are in business and if we don't make money, we can't do anything for society. So we strategically invest in the growth and development of our workforce."

As CCO, Taylor oversees the company's altruistic interests and community-based programs, all of which aim to enrich and improve the communities where the company does business. With a résumé that includes time as the president and CEO of the Los Angeles Urban League and president of the retail franchising company COI/ICD, Taylor is uniquely positioned at the intersection of private and public collaboration. I asked him to share the view from this vantage point during a conversation on one of his rare days off the road and at the office in Seattle.

Though Taylor is obviously a proponent of private sector engagement and collaboration with its sister sectors, in his telling this is a bit of a lonely road for Starbucks. "We are all too often the only company in the room in the meetings I attend," he sighs. "It's concerning because jobs are the end, not training or even education. We have to get people into positions of employment and on a career track with companies. And unfortunately the people with the jobs to give are not present."

To do its part, Starbucks announced in 2014 that it would cover tuition costs in forty different programs for employees who enroll in and complete their degrees at Arizona State University, whose online degree program is considered one of the best in the nation. This new program offers counseling and coaching support to help students navigate the learning process. Employees don't have to pay Starbucks back if they leave.[75]

Strategies like that one acknowledge that demand for talent is rising rapidly across the nation. This is a welcome response from a large employer—Starbucks employs roughly 135,000 people in the United States—in a way that helps the company do well and do good.[76] They clearly help their own employees, many of whom already have attended college but have nothing to show for it because they dropped out or stopped out. They help themselves as a business by educating some portion of their own future leadership ranks. And they help the communities where they operate, because many of those people will end up leaving Starbucks but staying in those communities, impacting not only those towns and cities but, in a modest way, the entire nation.

But Taylor, sounding a Paul Revere–like cry, sees that America's human capital, its untapped talent, if left uncultivated, could transform into something of an economic time bomb. "Young people who are working and have income buy products and homes, and will be contributing members of society and, of course, will be customers of ours," he notes, in an ideal outcome. "But if this does not happen, we are talking about a population that is so big it could topple the global economy. We are talking about 300 million young people, who are the future of the global economy. If we don't get our arms around that, the future of America does not look so bright."

Private employers like Starbucks have an important role in getting us to the higher level of talent we crave and avoiding the crisis scenario Taylor mentions. But what if we also saw our nation's cultural institutions—the thousands of museums, libraries, and performing arts organizations—as part of the national talent development framework? What if, in addition to colleges and universities, workplace-based training, and military or civilian service, we saw these cultural institutions as core elements of our formal talent development network?

Take libraries, for example. In my view, libraries have always been on the cutting edge of change. Many people may think that a library's main function is preservation, not disruption—that it serves as a repository, not as a laboratory. I would challenge that view. Any good library must be a good archive, but that's just the beginning. What really matters is that the archive point the way to new knowledge, inspiring and enabling genuine learning.

A good example is the New York Public Library (NYPL), which has recently taken steps under its dynamic president, Tony Marx, to focus its work more intentionally as a learning institution. NYPL has ninety-two branches across New York City with more than eighteen million people annually taking advantage of its services.[77] The library has all of the features we'd come to expect of an entity that fosters and recognizes talent—tremendous learning resources, a highly talented staff of professionals who are schooled in learning and knowledge development, and a mission (inspired by our old friend Andrew Carnegie) to make knowledge and information accessible to all.

If NYPL decided to formally take on the challenge of recognizing talent, it might use its substantial resources to either issue its own learning credentials, or establish collaborations with other entities to do so. Private capital—including from private foundations that have the leadership responsibility I mentioned earlier—could be invested to help build out this capacity while ensuring that the core mission of the library continues to grow. This "buy, don't make" strategy would give the nation a significant advantage by adding a new capacity to a well-established and proven learning enterprise.

Museums also can get in the game. The American Museum of Natural History in New York has long granted a PhD in comparative biology, and more recently added a master's degree in teaching science.[78] A recent announcement of expansion at the museum hints that it may be building capacity to do even more in the post–high school education realm.[79]

The evolutionary transformation of existing institutions—whether they be colleges and universities, employers, or cultural institutions—is one key tool that can be fashioned to unleash private sector innovation at a scale that could meaningfully impact the talent profile of the country. And ensuring that private capital is used to both transform existing entities and promote the creation of entirely new modalities is an opportunity, though one that neither government nor the private sector can tackle independently. What will be required is a new mindset, a different orientation.

The emerging movement known as social enterprise or social innovation represents a unique though still largely untested tool for advancing America's talent. Social enterprise is a strategy to use business or commercial means to advance social—human, environmental—outcomes. In a social enterprise, profit is still possible: Some social enterprises are legally structured as for-profits, others as nonprofits, and still others as "public benefit" corporations. But any excess capital is typically not returned to shareholders unless the social goals have been met. The return on investment for investors of varying types is still possible, and in many cases preferred, but is superseded by the goal of achieving the social outcome.

This type of social innovation is desirable in the drive to increase American talent, because we are stuck in a rut. As noted earlier in this book, some important innovations are clearly in play right now, like competency-based learning, which could transform the landscape of US talent if implemented at scale. But finding the best ways to bring those models to their maximum potential, while ensuring that we not crater the best of what already is being done, is complex.

Consider the fact the many well-intentioned efforts have been made in the past couple of decades to advance the nation's talent levels, from federal government programs to private ventures. Most recently, in 2014, the Congress reauthorized the Workforce Investment Opportunity Act, a longstanding federal effort aimed at helping workers improve their workplace-based talent, especially those at the lower end of the skill scale.[80] It took a decade to reauthorize this law, which, while important, represents only about $3 billion in investment per year. Even with a high degree of efficient and effective investment, those resources won't make much of a dent in the talent deficit.

What is needed is a two-pronged strategy to get much greater results from both public and private investment, using the power of private capital as the spark.

The first prong is to *establish new entities that can help create a talent dividend for the nation.* These can serve as complements to the existing entities already working on this task—nonprofit colleges and universities (both public and private), training organizations, for-profit educational institutions, and others—but in need of major modernization and upgrading (as discussed earlier).

A number of corporations and businesses have made it a priority to pursue various social goals in concert with their revenues. This is not an informal pledge to do good, but rather an incorporated commitment—several states have passed laws allowing companies to certify themselves as public benefit corporations. It's a binding agreement. If the business in question fails to pursue and pay attention to the cause it has committed itself to, shareholders can sue or remove the entity's leaders and directors.

B Corps, as they are called, are not new. But their existence and more recent proliferation is a good example of how social goals and profit-making motives need not be diametrically opposing forces. Companies in the retail sector, such as Ben & Jerry's and Patagonia, and various entities in the knowledge/tech sectors (including the publisher of this book, RosettaBooks), have advanced the notion that doing well and doing good are increasingly important in today's highly connected, socially challenged world.

B Corps are in essence a deconstruction of the false dichotomy between the for-profit and nonprofit universes. This has important implications for building talent nationally. Early experiments have already been undertaken. For example, Rasmussen College changed its status to a public benefit corporation in 2014 after nearly a century of experience as a traditional for-profit entity.[81] While these types of conversions are a start, the real opportunity is in the creation of wholly new B Corps that see the social mission as their *raison d'être* at the onset, not something to retreat to because of regulatory or other pressures.

An entity already exists to help support the development of standards for these B Corps, called B Lab. Based in Pennsylvania, B Lab works on building infrastructure and ecosystems to help people distinguish between companies that are doing good and those that are merely good at marketing. Public benefit corporations are legal entities that can consider the interest of all stakeholders, including students, when making business decisions; in contrast, regular C Corporations are required to maximize shareholder value.

To build a transparent marketplace that is driven by both financial performance and social impact, there must first be broadly accepted metrics that comprehensively measure effectiveness. B Lab has built a common set of social and environmental performance standards and an evaluation platform, called the B Impact Assessment, which are used to measure a company's performance within several different categories, in areas like governance, workers, community, and environment, as well as how the overall business model affects intended beneficiaries.

These performance standards undergird a variety of activities that B Lab oversees, including helping businesses to get the formal designation as a "benefit corporation" from Delaware and several other states that are beginning to understand this dual role of creating both shareholder and social value. B Lab also issues its own corporate certification to recognize companies that are meeting higher standards of social performance, accountability, and transparency.

To date, more than 15,000 companies, including Laureate Education in the area of higher education, have used B Lab's free, proprietary standards to benchmark their general, non-industry-specific performance; to attract social investment capital; and to identify, develop, and manage key supply chain relationships.[82]

B Corps might even have a role to play in attracting talent. Ryan Honeyman, an expert who literally wrote the book on the subject (*The B Corp Handbook: How to Use Business as a Force for Good*), notes that being a B Corp can give a company a way of differentiating itself from others competing for the same talent. "Becoming a Certified B Corporation can unleash the passion, initiative, and imagination of employees by connecting them with the larger purpose behind their work," says Honeyman.[83]

The second prong is to *develop and deploy new financing mechanisms to actually get the results desired*—in this case, a more talented American society capable of meeting our economic and social goals. New financing mechanisms come and go, but one intriguing financial tool that has gained considerable attention is a Social Impact Bond (SIB). A SIB is an incentive contract that enables a contracting party to pay for performance and shift the risk that a program may not achieve the desired social outcome to an outside investor. Social Impact Bonds involve three parties representing all three sectors of the economy—government, nonprofit, and business.

The contracting party promises to pay a fixed amount for a desired social outcome (for example, increasing the number of students who receive post-secondary degrees). The investor agrees to accept payment from the contracting party for delivering the social outcome. The service provider, with whom the investor contracts, performs the service that generates the outcome for which the investor receives payment from the contracting party. SIBs are attractive in meeting our talent needs because they focus on outcomes, can encourage government efficiency, deploy capital, amplify impact, and foster collaboration.

SIBs are complicated mechanisms, and there's been a fair amount of confusion over them, especially in the US (they were developed in the UK, with the first SIB issued in 2010), where the term "bond" has caused some consternation. To be clear, these are not bonds in the traditional sense, because the roles of the players in a traditional bond deal (the holder/lender and the issuer/borrower) are not as clear-cut. Still, they are intriguing as a financing approach because they focus both the holder and issuer on the idea of achieving a social outcome, rather than the traditional idea of generating interest.

US lawmakers are even getting in on the act. Todd Young, an Indiana congressman whose district reaches from the southern edge of Indianapolis to the Ohio River, traveled to England to study the effectiveness of SIBs.[84] Upon his return to Washington, Young, a Republican, teamed with Maryland Democrat John Delaney to introduce HR 4885 in 2014, also known as the Social Impact Bond Act, which would fund SIBs at the federal level.[85] The bill did not advance before the new Congress took over.

Even so, it's not clear that a federalized approach to SIBs is the answer. My gut says that federal legislation on this subject is probably premature. At the same time, it helps to have a straw man bill as a way to get some discussion going, and possibly even to support some modest demonstration programs. Ultimately, testing of these mechanisms is a best, first step.

This combination of strategies—relying on the leadership of employers and philanthropy to actively participate in talent development at scale; tapping the capacities of cultural institutions like libraries and museums as formal participants in the talent development enterprise; creating new, innovative organizations that draw from the best practices and strategies of for-profit companies without making profit the primary motive; and developing new financing mechanisms to fund specific talent outcomes—could yield the kinds of dividends that will materially impact the nation's talent needs. Much of this is relatively untested, to be sure, and will require some experimentation and refinement. But these new ways of unleashing private sector innovation to increase American talent are surely worth exploring, given the chasm that exists with our current approaches.

7

US DEPARTMENT OF TALENT

I know, I know. We don't need to add yet another agency to the current federal bureaucracy. That's not what I have in mind.

Let's get back to one of the biggest barriers we face in getting to a more talented society. Government. We've already discussed two of the Five Ways that will lead the nation to a greater talent dividend— rethinking what higher education is and does, and using the power of private capital markets to create a more innovative environment for talent development and deployment. But to solve society's biggest talent problems, we need government policy to align with those and other efforts, all working in a coordinated way, and capitalizing on the strengths of each. This is easier said than done.

Though government is not always the solution to our nation's biggest challenges, it is clearly one tool in the toolbox. The federal government, in particular, can have a unique impact on national priorities when it operates effectively, efficiently, and with clear goals and outcomes. That's because the federal government is well positioned to address the national talent needs of a mobile, interdependent society.

History has shown that there are many examples of federal government policy success—if success is defined as achieving the intended outcome to support the public good at a reasonable cost. At the federal level, the GI Bill, Clean Air Act, workplace discrimination laws, rural electrification, and the Centers for Disease Control and Prevention are examples that readily come to mind.

Of course, many government policies fail as well, and that is what makes policy making so complex and frustrating. The experience of the past few decades, in particular, is truly a mixed bag. For every policy area that has been a success, we can point to a glaring example of policy that has failed completely. For every GI Bill, Social Security program, or Interstate Highway System, there is a corresponding scheme that either failed to produce its stated outcome or had difficulty demonstrating what exactly works. The outcomes and impact of the well-intentioned and much-loved early childhood education program Head Start, for example, have been difficult to discern. A study published in 2010 by the US Department of Health and Human Services, which houses and administers the program, revealed that the positive impact it has on children vanishes by their first full year of school.[86] With an annual investment of more than $7 billion, it's not unreasonable to ask what we can do better to help make this admirable program stronger and ultimately more successful.

In this particular case, it's worth noting that Acelero, a New York-based organization founded by Aaron Lieberman, a former Head Start teacher, has made inroads in both improving and articulating the program's outcomes. Acelero is in essence a Head Start turnaround. They take over struggling Head Start centers, which are traditionally run through donations and by volunteers. In contrast to this model, Acelero brings a for-profit approach to the program. Its centers in New Jersey, Nevada, and Pennsylvania don't actually profit from Head Start dollars, but by running the program more efficiently, it can wring savings and then profit through state subsidies for "wraparound" services—features of Head Start centers that extend beyond their traditional three-and-a-half-hour class time, such as day care.[87]

The result has thus far been improved facilities, better pay for staff, more effective management, and merit pay for teachers. The model holds some promise in reforming a program desperately in need of change. And the early data shows that the promise is not misplaced: According to Rutgers' National Institute for Early Education, children attending the Acelero Head Start have had two to three times the gains in literacy and three to five times the gains in math skills as those enrolled in the traditional Head Start model.[88]

Structured as the federal government is—unable to respond in a timely way to market forces, slow to change or adapt or even address its own structural deficiencies—it's hard to conceive the federal government as being capable of meeting the enormous demand for talent, despite some encouraging signs. Even when solutions are out there, on a federal level, they are very hard to implement.

Martha Kanter, whom we heard from earlier, is the former chancellor of one of the largest community college districts in the nations—the Foothill–De Anza Community College District in California—a member of the faculty at New York University, and spent five years in the federal Department of Education. As undersecretary of Education, the nation's top federal higher education official, Kanter encountered many of the obstacles to progress on the federal level, no matter the party running the show or its objectives.

"Government is not fully designed for success. At least half of teacher preparation regulations, for example, make no sense anymore," she confessed when I talked with her nearly a year after she returned to academia. "We don't have the will to remove any more layers. It's just calcified. We have not focused enough on collaboration over competition." She cited the lack of synchronicity and teamwork in Washington. "There is so much competition internally in the government. It's hard to execute."

Candid, troubling, and true.

So where do we sit when it comes to federal policy related to talent development and deployment? The answer is complex to decipher—and that's exactly the problem. For every high-quality outcome we can point to—like the higher rates of low-income student access to higher education as a result of the Pell Grant program—we can point to equal efforts that have failed. An example can be found in the case of the US Department of Labor's One-Stop Job Centers, an all-in-one resource for employment seekers intended to guide potential applicants toward available jobs and educate them on, among other things, how to obtain the necessary skills to find a niche in the workplace.[89] The Hamilton Project, an initiative of the Brookings Institution, has pointed out that while these are effective programs that connect citizens with jobs, they have been frustrated by federal regulations and improper allocation of funds; as a consequence, too many workers have failed to locate and lock in on the right opportunity.[90]

Yet even in these cases, the successes of programs like Pell Grants can mask their shortcomings (inability to serve the growing eligible population, failure to focus on student success) while conversely the failings of approaches like One-Stop Centers might actually point to their possible successes (serving fifteen million unemployed, trying to link programs and services).[91]

Beyond the uncertainty of outcomes across programs and policies, we can also point to the incomplete nature of some policies. Pell, for example, has been a great success in helping those low-income students—many of them minority, or first-generation college attenders—get into college. But is getting *into* college our only goal as a society? Don't we actually want those students to gain value from the access they've gained? Shouldn't they be *completing* college and demonstrating that they've learned things that can help them be successful in the workplace, and in life?

The evidence here is decidedly less clear. In 2013, an analysis supported by both Lumina Foundation and the Bill & Melinda Gates Foundation determined that the intentions and ends of the Pell Grant program were not fully aligned, serving two distinct and unconnected populations with different goals (the traditional college student and adults over twenty-four), and often resulted in disappointing completion rates.[92] Clearly this is an example of a well-intended federal policy in need of redesign.

Adding to the uncertainty is that these policy efforts are truly atomized. What the US Department of Education does in terms of its postsecondary education programs has little or no relation to what the US Department of Labor might do, and even less to what the Immigration Service thinks or does about talent.

Unfortunately, this isn't a new problem. Over the course of several decades, and with different parties controlling both Congress and the White House, this issue of poor coordination and collaboration across agencies has surfaced time and again. In the mid-1990s, Republican Congressmen William Goodling and Steve Gunderson proposed a merger of the US Departments of Labor and Education. Their proposal was primarily aimed at efficiency—reducing investment at a time when the nation clearly needed to ramp up its efforts to improve worker capacity. Then Labor Secretary Robert Reich (whose autobiographical book *Locked in the Cabinet* is a telling example of the frustrations of being in government, even as a member of the president's inner circle) rightly opposed this merger, saying in testimony that the proposal would neither save money nor improve services, a reasonable conclusion at the time.[93]

Merging such complex agencies *en masse* is a bad idea. Think about combining the relatively focused US Department of Education, which works to improve access to education for underserved populations and helps prepare students for both work and life, with the immense mission of the Labor Department, which not only focuses on workforce preparation but also labor standards, unemployment insurance, worker health and safety, and a range of other services.

Mashing the Department of Labor with the Department of Education would be messy, time-consuming, and probably fruitless. Yet even Reich has acknowledged that there is a serious flaw with the fact that there is a Labor Department focused on workforce preparation as one of its core goals and an Education Department where workforce preparation is a relatively small budget item. In his 1992 book *The Work of Nations*, Reich argued that a country like the United States has two main resources to define its success—infrastructure (like roads and telecommunications systems) and workers. The capacity of workers to contribute to national success hinges on their ability to meaningfully contribute to both their own success and the national economic and social fabric of the country, Reich suggested. And yet investment in education and "training" was disconnected from this reality, with the separate policies and systems led by Education and Labor rarely connecting. Shouldn't there be better coordination between the two, Reich reasoned?[94]

Maddeningly, little has changed in the two decades since Reich offered that advice. Indeed, in the first term of the Obama administration, a high-ranking and respected education policy leader, Jane Oates, served as assistant secretary of Labor overseeing the critical Employment and Training Administration, among other key Labor Department responsibilities. She led with conviction and purpose, doing well with the hand that she was dealt. Yet despite Oates' considerable talent in the education space—from her experience as Senator Ted Kennedy's chief education adviser, and as commissioner of Higher Education in the state of New Jersey—the discord between Labor and Education was little changed.

My own experience in Washington over the course of two decades was that there was little collaboration, if any, between these two mega-agencies, or with others. Sure, various interagency task forces and working groups were (and still are) created, but the net result of that collaboration is hard to visualize at a macro level. Today, when we talk about the impact of federal policy on meeting labor force needs, for example, we rarely make reference to the Pell Grant program, even though it is an enormously important investment in talent development that can power our economy and strengthen our democracy (roughly $32 billion in Pell Grants were awarded to students in 2013).[95] But because it is seen as an education program—one that is clearly and unequivocally the purview of only the US Department of Education— there are precious few examples of ways in which this key program can be said to directly drive the increasing talent development of the nation. To do so would be considered dangerous by the advocates of the Pell program, who frequently tell me that they worry it could become conflated with "lesser" efforts like the job training programs of the Labor Department.

So what's the solution? What's needed is an agency that does two things really well. The first is that it can be clear about its goals, how policies align with those goals, and then can report honestly and accurately about what works, and what doesn't.

The second is that it has both the capacity and the authority to cut through the red tape, the bureaucratic turf protecting, and the collective noise of competing constituencies.

No current federal agency can solve these problems on its own. The sum has to be greater than the parts. The only way we will ever get to a truly coordinated national talent strategy is to make sure that the people who control the allocation of resources and policy implementation responsibilities actually work together.

What should be included in this new Department of Talent? Avoiding the wonkish issues of congressional committee jurisdiction (turf is a real impediment to change) and agency capacity, I'd propose three main entities as a starting point:

- the current functions of the US Department of Education in their entirety;

- the Employment and Training Administration (ETA) of the US Department of Labor; and

- the talent recruitment functions of the US Citizenship and Immigration Service (USCIS) under the Department of Homeland Security.

Why these entities? Let's start with the most obvious, which is the Education Department. It doesn't make a lot of sense to slice off parts of this agency—all of its work is aimed at developing and deploying a diverse pool of talent for the nation, from early childhood through adult education. Indeed, the current mission statement of the Department of Education makes this point clearly: "to promote student achievement and preparation for global competitiveness by fostering educational excellence and ensuring equal access."

Including ETA from the Labor Department is critical because it administers federal job training and worker dislocation programs, federal grants to states for public employment service programs, and unemployment insurance benefits. These services are primarily provided through state and local workforce development systems.

Meanwhile, the US Citizenship and Immigration Service is home to the Entrepreneurs in Residence Program, an online reference for American employers and foreign talent. Its purpose is to generate feedback from the business community on its staffing needs and to provide skilled immigrants with the information to navigate the visa application process. This program also contains start-up training, workshops, and libraries for immigration officers. In other words, it's an effort to sync the needs of the business community to the potentially available overseas talent and encourage that talent pool to come to America with the promise of a streamlined immigration policy. Great. But is it not odd that this function would be housed in the same federal apparatus—the Department of Homeland Security—as ICE (Immigration and Customs Enforcement), which is also responsible for enforcement and deportation?

Getting this function out of Homeland Security also helps to fix a serious mixed message that now exists. ICE's job is heavily weighted toward enforcing the immigration laws and regulations that are critical to our national economic and social security. With USCIS housed in the same agency, DHS is in the odd position of granting the rights to visit or stay in the United States through visas, green cards, and other mechanisms.

If you want visual proof, take a look at the ICE home page and you'll see that the news ticker is replete with stories about catching predators, violent offenders, and drug traffickers. Sometimes these headlines are hard to distinguish from the headlines that welcome students and others to study in the US. The mix of law enforcement and national security protections simply doesn't mesh with strategies designed to meet the nation's broad needs for talent.

In addition to these three core agencies, a fourth, the Office of Head Start now in the US Department of Health and Human Services (HHS), might also need to be considered for inclusion, given how important Head Start could be to the school readiness of vulnerable children. This is a more complex nut to crack, in part because Head Start is tightly intertwined with other benefit programs housed in the Administration for Children and Families at HHS.

A US Department of Talent would bring about the possibility of several important outcomes. One is greater efficiency and focus. Think about an agency that could develop and implement strategies for linking standards-driven K–12 education (taking the lead from states, irrespective of whether they are formally implementing the hotly debated Common Core education standards), high-quality, locally managed workforce development programs, and highly focused global recruitment strategies for meeting the nation's workforce gaps in areas where we literally can't produce the talent fast enough, or in some cases cheaply enough.

Greater efficiency also ties to the issue of effectiveness—the actual success of the programs and strategies being managed by the agency. A US Department of Talent would tie together approaches that have been disconnected, and bureaucratically entrenched, and replace them with ones focused on outcomes. The net result would be an agency actually aimed at the true outcome of the policies inherent in the current disconnected mess—talent—rather than an agency that is focused on processes and tools like "education," "training," "visas," etc.

Former Massachusetts governor and presidential contender Mitt Romney famously spoke about his desire to staple a permanent resident card on every foreign college graduate's diploma.[96] The idea, simply put, was to keep the talent we helped create in our colleges and universities—a fairly unobjectionable idea on its own. Yet within that idea lies a host of questions that would be difficult for an agency that issues visas to answer. In what areas does the United States have workforce shortages, now and in the foreseeable future, that would be best served by issuing such visas? How do these foreign student graduates compare to the talent being developed in our own citizens? Shouldn't an agency that has a better sense of our talent needs be positioned to assess workforce shortages and thereby make decisions about immigration status?

Consolidating and repurposing agencies is not without precedent, either in the US context or globally. When the Corporation for National and Community Service was created in the early 1990s (I played a small role in that work as a consultant and adviser to the senior leaders of the corporation), it included both new programs and existing efforts. The nascent AmeriCorps, aimed at getting greater individual commitment to national service via community-based programs, was brought together with existing programs like VISTA, which is primarily devoted to building organizational and financial infrastructure for community-based nonprofit organizations. The merger and refocusing has led to a true national service movement, one where hundreds of thousands of individuals have participated, where both new and existing nonprofit organizations have successfully served those individuals and the social needs of communities.

Internationally, several countries have created agencies that link together both knowledge transmission—education and training—with knowledge development, in areas like technology, scientific achievement, innovation, etc. One example is Kenya's Ministry of Higher Education, Science, and Technology, which oversees everything from teacher training, to schoolhouse bricks and mortar, to childhood education, to higher education, to polytechnic training. Poland, South Sudan, Slovenia, and South Korea, just to name a handful, have similar agencies.

In America's federal government, we have seen agencies move *away* from collaboration and consolidation. "There was some beauty in having a Health, Education, and Welfare department," Martha Kanter told me. That agency, which closed in 1979, gave way to separate federal departments, one for Education and one for Health and Human Services, and, as a result, created more layers of bureaucracy as well as the competition Kanter mentioned earlier.

But what if we reversed this formula in pursuit of talent?

A US Department of Talent would send a powerful message to the people of the United States, employers, and our global partners and competitors that the federal government is serious and strategic about its interest in developing, harnessing, and deploying talent in the country. It also would send a message about government and its potential to do good, if properly focused and aimed at clear results. Mitch Daniels, former Office of Management and Budget director, Indiana governor and fiscal conservative hero—whose current assignment is as university president—was fond of saying during his gubernatorial tenure that he didn't want to eliminate all government; he wanted to make sure that we have the government we actually need. As he put it in his typically blunt way at a 2011 speech to the Conservative Political Action Committee, "We should distinguish carefully skepticism about Big Government from contempt for all government."[97] The US Department of Talent might be one small step to show that government can work in a way that serves our shared interests as a country.

8

IMMIGRATION, INNOVATION, INSPIRATION

Immigration is a core part of the story of American success. After all, we are a nation of immigrants, built on and constantly renewed by the energy and innovation of a diverse population. Indeed, my own family story is not unlike the story of millions of Americans. We are an immigrant family; my mother, Diana Stafilarakis, was born on the island of Crete in Greece in 1932 and immigrated to the US as a child. Her family had arrived more than a decade earlier, only to sour on the American experience and return to Greece. They made the trip back a few years later, however, as limited job opportunities in Greece presented themselves in the pre–World War II global Depression era, and as the tug of a better life in America drew both my grandparents and my mother's oldest siblings back.

My father's parents immigrated to New Hampshire just a few years before he was born in 1922. My dad, Peter Merisotis, the oldest of four children born to Ernest and Athena Merisotis, is in many ways the classic 20th century "greatest generation" immigrant American. Though he was born in the US, he learned to speak Greek before he spoke English, and in my view was and is the model of a smart, hardworking immigrant whose drive and perseverance made it possible to raise a large family. My mother, my brothers Michael, Christopher, and Emanuel, and me, my father's mother, Athena, and (at times) one of his sons from a prior marriage all lived a stable, lower-middle-class lifestyle in the same two-bedroom home that he owned for more than forty years.

My dad dropped out of high school at the age of sixteen, choosing to earn money to help out his dad, who had taken a second mortgage on their home during the height of the Depression. Dad was able to use his talent as a guitarist and mandolin player—learned from his father—and joined a traveling group called Ken MacKenzie's Hill-Billy Tent Show to help bring money home.

A few years later, however, he was conscripted into the war and found himself as the tail gunner and radio operator on a B-24 Liberator—the youngest man doing the most dangerous job on the plane. He was shot down in the European theater in 1944, held prisoner for nineteen months, and finally returned home in 1945, ready to begin his life as a working adult in the new postwar economy.

Rather than take advantage of the GI Bill, Peter Merisotis chose instead to try his luck in a new city—Manchester, Connecticut, a working-class suburb of Hartford—in a state he had been to only once before. After a few years in odd jobs, working in a downtown luncheonette, doing some factory work, he finally settled into what would be his true calling: sales. Dad sold everything—encyclopedias, cosmetics, Fuller brushes—until he ended up in the field that, amazingly, would provide him with the means to support that family of seven-plus for more than thirty years.

Baby pictures.

Seriously. My father was the guy who showed up at your house with the free picture you had taken of your child at the local department store, and would try to sell you extra prints. If it sounds crazy and impossible, we always thought the same thing when we were kids. But that's what he did. With just the power of his affable personality, his ethical demeanor, and his amazing drive to succeed, my father used his God-given talent to make ends meet—sometimes just barely—until he was well into his seventies. Combined with the money my mother earned after returning to work in her forties, my parents raised a family, put their kids through school, and led productive, happy lives.

The Merisotis story, personalized as it is to reflect the unique personalities and character of one family, is not an unusual story of America in the past century. The immigrants of the 20th century arrived on these shores with energy and guts but often little in the way of cultivated talent or advanced education. Despite this, through hard work and hustle, they were able to carve out a place in America, provide for and raise families, and change the American landscape for the better.

But the 21st century is a far different ball game. God-given talent like my dad's, determination, and energy alone will no longer open doors or compensate for a lack of certain indispensable skills. It's worth asking: How would our immigrant grandparents and parents have fared in the current America? Without the proper training, likely not as well, and that would mean a radically different and far less successful and prosperous America.

Since historic times, cosmopolitan cities have enjoyed greater prosperity as they benefited from the fusion of ideas and skills from different cultures and peoples. The United States has long been a beneficiary of these forces as groups of immigrants from all over the world have made their home here and contributed to the prosperity of the country. Researchers have found that between 1870 and 1920, during the age of mass migration in the United States, the nation experienced significant increases in economic output.[98] In more recent times, researchers have observed a robust correlation within US metropolitan areas between the increase in the share of foreign-born population and growth in wages of US-born citizens, between 1970 and 1990.[99]

What's more, credible research shows that diversity, derived from historic patterns of immigration, breeds talent. The demographic makeup of the US labor force is changing quickly and profoundly. By 2050, if not sooner, whites will no longer be the majority of our workforce. This growing diversity offers substantial benefits for the US economy. In fact, a good deal of academic analysis shows that racial diversity enhances economic productivity of US cities.[100]

Figure 6. By 2050 Whites Will No Longer Make Up the Majority of the Labor Force

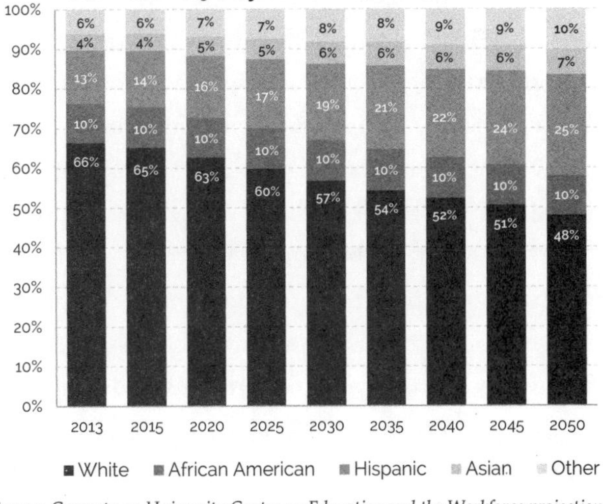

Source: Georgetown University Center on Education and the Workforce projection of labor force makeup by race/ethnicity, 2014

Research also shows that racial, ethnic, and gender diversity is associated with better organization/firm performance at the micro level and greater economic prosperity at the macro level. At the level of a firm or business, racial diversity has been shown to be associated with increased sales revenue, larger numbers of customers, greater market share, and greater relative profits.[101] Gender diversity has been shown to be associated with more customers, increased revenue, and greater profits.[102] In addition, firms with high representation of women on boards of directors and in senior management demonstrate better financial performance than firms with low shares of women or no women in those positions.[103]

Firms with greater gender and racial/ethnic diversity have also been found to be more likely to innovate, apply for more patents, and have greater breadth of patents in technological fields.[104, 105] Cultural and racial diversity benefits firms with enhancing their growth strategy, leading to improvements in productivity, return on equity, and market performance.[106] There's also evidence of a positive linear relationship between diversity and firm performance over the long-term.[107]

"One mechanism behind the success of diverse organizations appears to be the greater capacity of diverse groups to adeptly solve problems and make effective decisions. If you take a racially and ethnically diverse group of problem solvers randomly drawn from a large group of problem solvers who meet

Figure 7. Higher Racial and Gender Diversity Corresponds to Greater Sales Revenue for Businesses

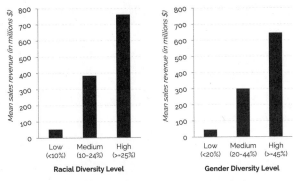

Source: Herring, Cedric. "Does Diversity Pay? Race, Gender, and the Business Case for Diversity." American Sociological Review, 74, no. 2, (April 2009), Table 1, pg. 216; based on 1996–1997 National Organizations Survey (NOS) data

certain minimum ability standards, they can actually outperform a group of high-ability problem solvers—individuals drawn from the top of the ability-based distribution.[108] Diverse groups are better at avoiding groupthink, a phenomenon where members of the group refrain from expressing and considering contradictory opinions to avoid upsetting group cohesion.[109]

So what does this quick review of research tell us? Boiled down, I think it's clear that diversity has offered the nation important economic benefits at both the macro and micro levels and will play an important role in the US economy with the changing demographics of the workers and students.

But things have changed, and our ability to encourage greater diversity through immigration—and harness the energy and drive that immigrants bring to our shores—has been hampered by years of policy drift and outright hostility to even minor changes in the immigration system. This is important to keep in mind when we contemplate changes to that system.

Now, at this point you might think proposals to reform America's immigration laws are nothing new or novel. True. But if you have been paying attention to the ongoing national debate on this issue, you will know that so far every idea put forth, by both Democrats and Republicans, has either fallen flat or seriously backfired.

In fact, during the writing of this book, Congress was engaged in a tense but in many ways fruitless battle with President Obama over immigration reform. After what Obama said was too long of a wait on comprehensive reform, he took action using (what he believed was) his executive authority to clarify the status of millions of people who are living in the US without any legal standing. This got the federal courts involved. The nasty debate over immigration shows no signs of abating, nor does there appear to be a prospect for passing comprehensive immigration reform—action that would cover the continuum of talents that the United States desperately needs. At the moment, it looks like a no-go, at least until after the next presidential election. Even then, any reforms passed now will likely just be scratching at the surface of a major obstacle to America's economic well-being.

So I will be an opportunist and use this impasse as a forum to attempt to introduce what I hope is some different thinking on the subject.

First of all, a simple truth, restated: Immigrants have always been a crucial ingredient to our culture of hard work, inventiveness, and innovation, and that remains as true as ever.

Of course, immigrants come to the United States from hundreds of different countries, and this diversity is matched by the skills that accompany these new Americans. Analysts often use the terms "low-skilled" and "high-skilled" to draw a distinction between the credentials and education of those in question. But the truth is we need both skill sets and everything in between: Immigrants, no matter their qualifications, drive our economy.

And despite claims that incoming "low-skilled" workers take away wages from Americans, a study by the University of California, Davis revealed that immigration representing the full spectrum of talent has actually increased the national income of American workers by $5,400 a year.[110] At the far end of the talent spectrum, the United States benefits from the innovation and ingenuity that "high-skilled" immigrants bring to our shores. For example, *BusinessWeek* reported that between 2001 and 2010, British citizens living in the US applied for 14,893 patents. The number for Chinese citizens living here was even greater.[111] The point: America was and is still a beacon for the innovative and a staging ground for their dreams. But here is the unnerving reality: This stream of innovators and innovation may be drying up.

This would be tragic for the nation. The impact of immigrant innovators on America's economic, social, and cultural prowess will be severely hampered without the kind of welcoming, pro-growth philosophy that gave the nation its edge, innovators like Jan Vilcek, who came to the US in the mid-1960s as a defector from then-communist Czechoslovakia. Vilcek took an appointment at the New York University School of Medicine, using his position as professor of microbiology to study cytokines, proteins that play an important role in the immune system. His groundbreaking research on interferon, one of those immune system proteins, and other proteins subsequently led to the development of the anti-inflammatory drug Remicade, which has had a profound effect on the treatment of patients suffering from Crohn's disease, rheumatoid arthritis, and other types of inflammatory disorders. Vilcek has since used his scientific prominence and wealth to support other foreign-born scientists and artists who are contributing to US society through the nonprofit Vilcek Foundation.

In his book *The Immigrant Exodus*, Vivek Wadhwa, an Indian-born American software developer and entrepreneur, explains that the trend of businesses founded and run by immigrants in the United States, which emerged and intensified in the 1960s, is now trailing off.[112] Many are choosing to take their ideas and companies back home, elsewhere, or are just staying put in the first place. According to Wadhwa, new Silicon Valley–based companies launched by Chinese and Indian immigrants dropped from 52 percent in 2005 to 44 in 2011. Why? An economic downturn no doubt contributed to this, but so did—and this is crucial—overly complicated, unfair, arbitrary, and scattered US immigration policy. With other nations offering much more comprehensible and focused immigration procedures, the US is simply not as attractive to talent anymore.

The timing could not be worse. The fact is we need their innovation and ingenuity now more than ever. According to the Georgetown Center on Education and the Workforce, foreign-born Americans currently add over a trillion dollars to the economy in direct value added from labor, or about 15 percent of the economic value from all sources of labor. So it makes sense that when we discuss the need for more national talent, we would turn our attention to one of the best resources we have for it and conduct the conversation with an eye on how we make the United States the most attractive destination for global talent.

To do this, let's start by recognizing that immigration is, plainly, one of our best sources for talent. And let's also try to get past the ugly nature of this debate and examine what foreign-born workers already contribute to the nation's success.

As with all workers, the ability of foreign-born workers to add value increases with their access to postsecondary education degrees. So, for example, foreign-born workers with bachelor's degrees and graduate degrees add the most value relative to their numbers. They represent 5 percent of our fellow workers, but add 8 percent to the valued added from labor in the American economy—more than $300 billion annually. Middle-skill foreign-born workers with associate degrees (or some college but no degree) represent 3 percent of workers and add an equivalent 3 percent economic value added from labor.

Foreign-born workers with high school or less, like all workers with that level of education, don't add economic value commensurate with their share of the workforce. High school dropouts, for example, are 4 percent of the population and contribute 2 percent of the wage share.

What's needed is a dual agenda for including the foreign-born in the talent society—an agenda that follows the path the nation took after World War II, but modernized to reflect our current needs and priorities. First, we need to repeat the post–WWII lessons of the American Century, when we lifted the children and grandchildren of the first great immigration wave into the middle class. European immigrant families who came here in the 1920s never really got going until their children and grandchildren moved into the middle class after World War II. Before World

War II, these populations were largely low-skill and low-wage. After 1946, the American immigrant story is closely tied to a huge surge in education, driven by Cold War politics and a deep understanding that we needed to be more highly educated to secure our newfound status as a global, technological, military, and economic superpower.

The education agenda for these already arrived immigrants is the subject of other parts of this book. The same changes in policy, delivery mode, and orientation have to apply to everyone. Failing to educate the immigrants already here, irrespective of how they arrived, just doesn't make sense.

Second, we need a skill-based immigration policy that recruits talent aggressively, across the skills spectrum, to meet our current and growing needs. We need to win the global contest for the most talented immigrants, just as we did after WWII, when we won the Cold War contest for German rocket scientists. Only this time, we need to do it on a much broader scale.

It's worth thinking about how we might make a skills-based immigration policy work. The lure of America has always been that your talents can be better applied in the context of social freedom and economic opportunity. I've thought about my own family's history, the experience of my mother and grandparents and what they were seeking here in America. While reviewing the Ellis Island records online about the Merisotis and Stafilarakis families, it was poignant to think about the powerful message that prospective Americans received about the nation's siren call to those seeking to apply their talents and build a better life. That message is perfectly embodied in Emma Lazarus' poem "The New Colossus" at the foot of the Statue of Liberty, which famously reads:

> *Give me your tired, your poor,*
> *Your huddled masses yearning to breathe free,*
> *The wretched refuse of your teeming shore.*
> *Send these, the homeless, tempest-tost to me...*

But I wonder if, in the 21st century, we should think about an addendum:

> *Send us your scientists, your doctors,*
> *Your educators and engineers,*
> *Your future Nobel Prize winners...*

We need to look at immigration in terms of the society we want to build; in terms of the skills and credentials we want Americans to have. So how do we refashion our immigration system accordingly?

The answer, believe it or not, may be found Down Under.

It's interesting to contemplate that the nation whose combination of immigration and education policies could serve to inspire our own was originally populated, in part, by immigrants who were, well, part of a penal colony.

That was then; this is now.

The Australian government has conceived immigration policies that, in terms of admission and visa status, favor immigrants who have the skills and education background that the country is looking for. In other words, a talent-based system.

Here's a snapshot of their system: Australia seeks skilled immigrants and encourages their migration. This is done partly through a points system that emphasizes and gives preference to potential citizens who possess certain skills the country is looking for, including (and prioritizing) employment experience and academic credentials.

This is all put into a calculator of sorts, with certain skills, especially those obtained in Australia, carrying a heavier weight for those seeking permanent residency. For example, a PhD is worth 20 points, a master's degree 15, and eight years of employment in Australia is worth 20 points.[113] One result is that the country gets the influx of talent it needs from immigration, and the newly arrived or minted Australians are folded into the national labor force—two major challenges conquered at the same time. A combination of a green card and a diploma, so to speak. And as a result, 25 percent of those enrolled in Australian schools are international students.

This program, or a variant of it, has been national policy since the 1970s. The net result is that Australia, as much or more than America, is a nation of immigrants: Since World War II, seven million migrants have found a home Down Under. The country has the second-highest number of foreign-born citizens in the world.[114]

US lawmakers should note that the Australian system is two-tiered. One component is supply-driven, giving priority to potential citizens whose skills and education match an employee profile the nation is looking for. The other side of the policy is demand driven, and takes into account what employment opportunities and industry needs. Under this system employers can sponsor migrants whose skill portfolios match those of open or needed jobs.

Supply is based on the Skilled Occupation Report, an annual study issued by Australia's Workforce and Productivity Agency, a rough equivalent to America's Department of Labor. This report indicates what skills the workforce needs and, by extension, who receives priority for visas. A second resource, SkillSelect, is an online venue where those interested in migrating to Australia can submit "expressions of interest." An applicant whose skills and education match an employer's needs receives an invitation to apply for a visa.

"It's not unlike an online dating service," jokes Janette Haughton, an immigration counselor at the

Australian Embassy in Washington. "But the approach ultimately broadens both our skills base and our demographics." The latter is a reference to Australia's aging population: By 2050, the number of retirees will grow by 137 percent, while the working population is projected to grow by only 59 percent.[115] An influx of younger, skilled workers can address this imbalance and its accompanying economic peril.

Indeed, according to Australia's census data, these policies have resulted in immigrants' accounting for a quarter of the Australian workforce. It also results, according to Mark Cully, the former chief economist for the Australian Department of Immigration and Citizenship, in a workforce made up of those who are young, more qualified and experienced, more fluent in English, and with skills in demand by employers. Meanwhile, a temporary work visa is available to other workers who wish to stay in the country for only up to four years. Individual states, such as sparsely populated South Australia and Tasmania, engage in their own recruitment.

Just as impressive as the focus of Australia's immigration policies is the speed at which they facilitate migration. Processing centers and coherent, simple checklists for applicants have reduced the wait time for receiving a visa from two years to sixty days. "Our system is designed to make the process as transparent and streamlined as possible," says Haughton. This makes an interesting contrast with the

American process, which can take anywhere from weeks to years.

Even in an economic downturn, there is no denying that America remains a choice destination for highly skilled immigration; there is not about to be a massive trailing off of the line of those who want to relocate and work here. But if the process is incoherent and lengthy, perhaps these would-be Americans will go elsewhere, especially to nations with easier-to-navigate immigration policies. "We know it's a competitive market," admits Haughton. "A doctor or scientist who is interested in going to the United States, but hears that it will take years to get a visa, might well look at other options, including Australia."

In addition to the streamlined process, Australia places a heavy emphasis within its point system on strong English language skills. It also has a somewhat more restricted interpretation of family than the US, where parents, siblings, and married sons and daughters may petition for green cards. Australia views family as simply spouse and children. This creates a mix that relies more heavily on talent. Of the 190,000 immigrants entering Australia per year, one-third are granted visas because of relations, the remaining two-thirds because of their skills.[116]

The net economic benefits of these policies are striking: Immigration has added nearly 2 percentage points to Australia's labor force participation rate over the past ten years.[117] It has neutralized the country's aging population by adding a surge of young workers through immigration. The new Australians, who are often high salary earners, also bolster Australia's budget by providing a new tax base. Combining all visa classes, in the year of arrival these immigrants added $3.4 billion to government budgets. By their twentieth year in the country, the number is $8.4 billion.[118] The fact that these new arrivals will have strong English language proficiency eliminates the need for language services, another efficiency.

This paints a promising picture, no doubt. Yet, despite a common language, there are many differences between Australia and America, chief among them population: At twenty-three million, Australia is actually home to fewer people than live in Texas. Still, the general ethos can provide inspiration and provide a focus for reform. Oddly, according to Haughton, US policy makers rarely if ever inquire about or study the Australian system. Perhaps this is because of the aforementioned perceived differences in the two nations, or, distressingly, perhaps it is the result of a myopic approach to policy making in this area that ignores the experiences of others.

Either way, the American immigration system is dysfunctional—if readers will pardon the overused terminology—and the political process by which it should be repaired is equally dysfunctional. That means potentially generations of talented Americans who should reach our shores, invent, build, and generate prosperity may actually never become Americans, and may end up innovating on another continent. That's a loss we can't afford.

The Australian system, with its focus, its efficiency, and its emphasis on skill, can't just be grafted onto our own. But if policy makers would take a second from their own debates on the subject and lend an ear to our friends Down Under, they may just find some inspiration, and, so importantly, start to rethink the subject not as a matter of fences and visas, but as the building block for the type of society we want to live in. It's worked in Australia; who's to say it won't work here?

One of the most insightful analysts of the failed US immigration system is Tamar Jacoby, a former *New York Times* editor who has made a name for herself as an advocate for sensible, comprehensive immigration reform. Jacoby has turned her gift for crisp, insightful analysis into a cottage industry of right-leaning thinkers who recognize that immigration reform and long-term economic and social success are integrally interconnected. I served on a bipartisan task force that Jacoby staffed in 2013 under the auspices of the Chicago Council on Global Affairs, and came to appreciate her ability to get to the point—sharply and unapologetically. In a 2014 analysis for the German Marshall Fund on point-based immigration systems, Jacoby wrote that these systems are key to economic advancement and social cohesion. "Instead of guessing about likely behavior, authorities would simply measure and reward it," she reasons.[119]

Tom Linebarger, chairman and CEO of Cummins, Inc., one of the world's largest manufacturers of diesel and natural gas engines—and a company that lists "social justice" as one of its three global priorities—recognizes the need for this kind of new thinking. He also acknowledges the enormousness of the challenge the US faces. Though Cummins is headquartered in Columbus, Indiana, the company, which has 48,000 employees, has facilities across the globe and does business in over 190 countries.[120] It needs employees who understand the cultures and customs of nations other than its own. Unsurprisingly, they recruit heavily from abroad.

But this, according to Linebarger, is a rocky road.

"People still want to live here. They still like the lifestyle, the freedoms, and the way our economy works. It all makes people excited to move here. But it's not easy to come here and it's getting more difficult," he laments. "If you are talented and have dreams, this is your place. We should not be making it more difficult. We should be making it easier."

Backing up those words, and not waiting for Washington to get its act together, if Cummins finds a recruit they believe will help their company, but who has a student visa instead of a work visa, they will handle the application process themselves. In some cases, if a visa is not obtained, Cummins will even help move the potential employee to a third country and apply again.

"Since when do we not want someone who is highly intelligent, makes $100,000 a year, and pays the taxes that go along with that salary living here?" asks Linebarger, incredulously. "It's good for Cummins and it's good for America."

Cummins' strategy for overcoming America's nonsensical immigration law is not too dissimilar, in spirit, from the principles that guide Australia's system. Think of the Cummins model as a domestic example of what has worked at scale in Australia.

The road from the optimistic, idealized days of America's Ellis Island immigration policy to today's convoluted, outdated, and ineffective one has been rocky. Immigration, like the people who are part of the process, is constantly changing, reflecting the evolving nature of society itself. Today's immigration policy must take a different path, one rooted in enhancing the talent needs of the country through a deliberate, skills-based policy model, while also using enhanced education policies to educate the immigrants who already have arrived. In either case, our immigration strategies must be focused on ensuring that we all benefit from the promise inherent in "The New Colossus" poem. These days, Ellis Island is a popular National Park Service site, and the inscription at the base of Lady Liberty is most often seen by tourists, not newly arrived immigrants. But the words still carry great meaning. It's time we applied them to the 21st century.

9

RESTORING THE RAPIDS—
CITIES AS TALENT HUBS

Since 2010, thirty-six American cities, towns, and municipalities have filed for bankruptcy.[121] Some of these were symbols of American industrial might and mid-20th-century prosperity. Today many of them are said to be going back to nature, Detroit being the most frequently cited example. Neighborhoods are deserted. Abandoned homes are overrun by weeds and wildlife. Once grand buildings, theaters, hotels, stadiums—sources of civic pride and centers of social engagement—are now cobwebbed and decrepit. Many of those with the wherewithal have long since left town. City government is ineffective, and sometimes even corrupt. And promises made to past and current employees as well as creditors go unfulfilled.

Welcome to the American city in the 21st century? Not necessarily. While some places have made incalculable management misjudgments and as a result are now facing the dire consequences, believe it or not, many American cities are headed in the opposite direction: up. And they are doing this by developing, attracting, and retaining talent.

Cities like Austin, Louisville, Syracuse, and others have taken a different turn, using their current talent, or the talent they can attract, as the key way to drive innovation, improve living conditions, and make the prospect of urban living not just tolerable, but vibrant.

The ability to get a good job and to make more money has important implications for cities. No one has been more eloquent on this point than the author Richard Florida, who has demonstrated that metro regions with high concentrations of "creative class" workers—people who are well educated, those who work in specific fields like technology, the arts, etc.—tend to have the highest levels of economic development. That economic development doesn't just come in abstract form, like a more favorable business climate. It has tangible benefits for individuals. In 2012, Florida published a short piece via *The Atlantic* called "America's Best Places for a Raise Since the Great Recession." What he showed was that those cities with the highest concentrations of college-educated workers experienced the greatest absolute increase in wages and salaries between 2006—before the recession began—and 2011. Raises were lowest for those cities with high concentrations of lower-skill, working-class jobs.[122]

Having a high concentration of college-educated workers is a good proxy for talent. But proxies aren't as valuable as the real thing. I began a quest to find an example of a thriving city that might not immediately spring to mind, but shows the powerful impact of proactively building a community with talent as the anchor for its civic and economic well-being. I concluded that one city that hasn't gotten enough credit for what it has done—but is emblematic of this resurgent notion that talent makes cities thrive—is Grand Rapids, Michigan. Some might be surprised by this choice, but in many ways it reflects the characteristics that Bruce Katz and Jennifer Bradley from the Brookings Institution describe in their groundbreaking 2012 book, *The Metropolitan Revolution*.

Katz and Bradley postulated a provocative theory: The dynamism, innovation, and future prosperity of America depend not on DC—which had hit bottom in 2012, and since then has shown signs of still digging— and not on states, but on our much-maligned cities. When I read the book, I was admittedly taken aback. By the authors' telling, places like Houston, Portland, and Denver are all going about their business growing, innovating, breaking through dysfunction, and making headway on all the issues—including immigration reform, equality of opportunity and income, political gridlock—that have bedeviled the nation's capital and its statehouses. Supreme Court Justice Louis D. Brandeis famously formulated that states were laboratories of democracy. Katz and Bradley instead suggest that the living labs now are actually our urban areas.

The changes that have taken place in Grand Rapids are the result of actions that cut across the public, private, and civic sectors. And while the project is not complete, the economic outcomes are decidedly encouraging, at all levels of the labor force.

Consider that the Grand Rapids metro area suffered more severe job loss during the recession than the US as a whole, according to the Metropolitan Policy Program at the Brookings Institution. The recession resulted in a nearly 9 percent loss in jobs compared to a 6 percent loss on the national level. Yet postrecession, the trend was reversed: During the recovery, Grand Rapids experienced a 16.7 percent increase in jobs. That far outpaced the 6.8 percent increase in jobs for the US as a whole.

Much of this postrecession boom in Grand Rapids has been in the two industries in which Grand Rapids specializes: manufacturing, and professional and business services. Both middle-skill jobs (many requiring a post–high school certificate or other credential, but not a bachelor's degree) and jobs requiring degrees grew substantially during the recovery, with manufacturing jobs increasing by roughly 25 percent and professional and business services jobs growing by about 42 percent. Other sectors in the Grand Rapids metro that have experienced relatively strong job growth post-recession include leisure and hospitality, and health services, also fields where higher skills are in demand but where the required level of formal learning varies from advanced postsecondary skills training to medical and other professional school education.

Before the recession, Grand Rapids had a higher unemployment rate than the national average. After the recession, the metro's unemployment rate is below the national rate: In the middle of 2014, Grand Rapids' unemployment rate was estimated at 5.4 percent, compared to the US rate of 6.2 percent.

Talent has clearly been a part of the renaissance of Grand Rapids, but how? In search of answers, I went, on Katz's recommendation, to Western Michigan. Grand Rapids had actually made an impression on me sometime before this sojourn. In 2011, *Newsweek* included the city on its list of dead or dying American metropolitan areas. In response, two citizens who didn't exactly concur with the magazine's assessment of their hometown raised $40,000, rallied the city, and produced a ten-minute video featuring huge crowds of locals walking, dancing, and singing through the streets of Grand Rapids while lip synching to Don McLean's "American Pie."[123] Called "the greatest music video ever made" by Roger Ebert, the Grand Rapids "lipdub" was an effective and moving response to the offending list, garnering more than five million YouTube hits.[124] And perhaps fittingly, it was *Newsweek* (in print form at least) that went under just a couple of years later, not Grand Rapids.

The video was a small but effective example of the can-do spirit and collaborative nature of the city.

"When I came here over 20 years ago this was a good town. But not a great town," says Birgit Klohs, the German-born president of The Right Place, Grand Rapids' leading economic development organization. Klohs—who acted as guide for my visit—and her organization have played a central role in the revitalization of the city.

Founded along the Grand River in the 1830s, Grand Rapids took advantage of its location (access to both transportation—the river—and ample resources in the form of raw materials) to build itself into a thriving community. By the turn of the 19th century, with over fifty furniture factories and the majority of its workforce employed in said factories, the city was a capital of that industry. It was even nicknamed "Furniture City USA."[125] But like so many of its neighbors with one product—Detroit and Flint, for example—when the companies moved south to North Carolina, Grand Rapids was staring into the abyss.

The notion of "hitting bottom" has been hard to characterize for Grand Rapids. But it certainly was not doing well for a very long time. From quality of life indicators, to school success, to the ways in which businesses recruited and retained talent, Grand Rapids was not thriving for much of the last half of the 20th century.

That's where Klohs and The Right Place, as well as many, many other organizations, most of them private, came into the picture; above all else, the Grand Rapids success story is one of teamwork.

"You wouldn't even have come down here two decades ago!" exclaimed Rick Chapla, a vice president at The Right Place. Chapla, a native Grand Rapidian, walked me through the city's buzzing streets on a sunny morning. Chapla points to neighborhoods that were previously vacant, or abandoned buildings that are now bustling homes to museums, restaurants, bars, loft apartments, colleges, and businesses. Many of these inhabit the former buildings of long-since departed companies. Even the town's towering Civil War monument (a sooty fixture in many Midwestern downtowns) is gleaming, the product of a recent restoration. Admittedly parts of Grand Rapids are still a work in progress—a number of the downtown's commercial areas still show patches of less-prosperous times—but it's hard not to get the impression that, unlike so many other municipalities, Grand Rapids is doing something very right.

"People come here and they ask us 'how did you do this?' and I tell them, these things just don't fall out of the sky," explains Klohs. "It takes entrepreneur-ship, it takes close collaboration, and it takes a vision from and for the community." The story she relates is one of constant experimentation, of private sector and nonprofit leadership working together to promote the city's goals, improve its quality of life, and make it an attractive place to call home. A perfect example is Grand Rapid's 12,000-seat entertainment venue, the Van Andel Arena. The $76 million cost of construction was raised by a cross-community partnership.[126] Today it's the thirteenth-most successful auditorium in the nation. "We have had everyone play here except the Rolling Stones and Paul McCartney," boasts Klohs.

Later I found myself in the office of the Grand Rapids Community Foundation, which, in keeping with the downtown's aesthetic scheme, is the historic site of an Anheuser-Busch bottling plant. On the floor above, a construction crew was commencing work on a new wing of the building, giving a noisy but real-time display of the city's rapid growth. Around the table sat a collection of city managers, including the mayor and other government officials, industry leaders, and representatives from public schools and community colleges.

Heads nodded as each participant talked up the community's culture of civic engagement and expec-tations that everyone gets involved, no exceptions made. It was an impressive picture. But, I asked, what does talent look like in Grand Rapids? What were all those around the table doing to bring it to and keep it in Western Michigan? And how was the community growing and retaining budding local talent?

"There is a disconnect between what comes out of the education system and what we need as employers," notes Fred Keller, the CEO of the Grand Rapids–based manufacturer Cascade Engineering. He points to credentialing, for example, echoing a national concern. "We need to know what people really know and employers need to describe what they need." It's a growingly familiar refrain. Traditional knowledge-based textbook learning is useful, but employers need employees with other skills and abilities. It's the only way to anticipate the needs of the future.

Here we come back to community collaboration. In Grand Rapids, there is an unspoken expectation that all community members, no matter the sector, step forward to solve the city's problems and meet its needs. The expectation is that entrepreneurship is not about temporary profits, but rather about creating businesses that will be part of the community and last for generations. Many of the companies in town are family owned. The business world (borrowing from academics) refers to this as social-emotional wealth: the idea that family businesses are more attuned to the needs not just of their stakeholders, but of their communities as well, and are focused on objectives other than profits. They invest in their communities because they are connected to them.

The perfect example, and the one most directly related to talent, comes from Herman Miller, a century-old family-owned but publicly traded furniture manufacturer based in Holland, Michigan, about thirty miles from Grand Rapids. Like so many companies along the Midwest's Rust Belt, Herman Miller was faced with the mass migration of young workers that was impacting its competitive position. Lacking a pipeline to replace them, in 2012 the company launched a program to place local high school students with Herman Miller employees. The goal is to impart business skills, and connect the students to possible positions in the company. In essence, it's an in-house university and vocational school.

The students come to the factories for half a day, working on the floor and in the offices, are assigned mentors, and become immersed in the culture at Herman Miller. In the first of the academy's two classes, twenty-one of twenty-two students graduated, and all but four went on to postsecondary schooling, either in Grand Rapids' community colleges or in four-year universities. When they return home in the summer they work for Herman Miller. At the beginning, when the first group was asked how many wanted to attend college, only three said yes.

According to Michael Ramirez, a senior vice president at Herman Miller, many parents were initially uninterested. "They thought it was child labor. 'What's your motive?' they asked," he recalls. But the company's employees were considerably more enthused. While they needed only twenty mentors, over 120 employees offered help. "This is a great opportunity for the kids and they are the group we need desperately to fill the gaps," says Ramirez.

Such a strategy is obviously good for the company, but it's also good for the community. And it's an excellent illustration of how cities and towns can cultivate, track, and place local talent and make sure it does not slip off to other locations. It's also an acknowledgment that employers have to play a greater role in informing young people of career paths, as even skilled teachers may not know what it looks like on the floor of an engineering plant and therefore can't expand the potential employment horizons of their students. Without the proper information and exposure, how can fifteen-year-olds match their ambitions and budding abilities to the appropriate industries?

The Herman Miller Academy, and its support from the Grand Rapids community, present a real solution to the disconnect between employers and K–12 education. And it's the start of a cradle-to-career pipeline in Western Michigan that can be replicated elsewhere. It's also an example of how the private sector is looking to schools to fill in the gaps in their employment needs. In typical Grand Rapids fashion, as Ramirez concludes his explanation of the academy, Kelly Savage, who handles human resources for Amway, instantly tells him: "If we are not helping you with that program, we would love to!"

Of course, Grand Rapids is not a finished project. Its public high school graduation rate has surged at double-digit rates in recent years, but is still well below the state average.[127] And while job creation has been part of the metro area's success, an aging and retiring workforce is creating a demand for workers and a shortage of qualified and willing candidates. But many parents continue to have uncharitable views of manufacturing jobs, according to the people I spoke with. Too often, their view of manufacturing is outdated, reflecting the view of a dusty, dark facility that is more reflective of the shop floor in the 1970s than it is today.

To combat this, and to make Grand Rapids more alluring to new workers and citizens, city leaders have worked to make quality of life improvements to the city—the Van Andel Arena, for example. Further confirming the culture of collaboration, local government has worked on a strong public transportation system, keeping streets clean and sidewalks full of people, and protecting and improving the environment, air, and water. It's all an effort to make Grand Rapids a place young people want to stay or come to and make their lives in.

Grand Rapids also is home to at least fifteen colleges and universities, which enroll more than 80,000 students. Unlike a typical college town, there is no single dominant institution of higher education in the city. There are law schools, culinary academies, bible colleges, and medical institutes. Many of them work to keep parents engaged, and to sell families on non-traditional education paths.

"It's impressive," offers John Engler, governor of Michigan from 1991 to 2003. Though he admits that it's still a struggle for cities like Grand Rapids to keep young talent, he sees much to praise. "They've figured out how to knit everything together; it's a continuum, from the medical and scientific sectors to the furniture industry to Amway, it's an educational ecosystem. And good things are happening."

So there it is, the metropolitan revolution in action. And while Grand Rapids' leaders and thinkers openly admit they have much work to do, they present a picture of a humming community where many organizations, no matter the sector, work together in harmony to translate the needs of the community into talent development. A place where new ideas are constantly being offered, vetted, improved upon, and implemented. And a community working hard to define what the American workforce looks like in the 21st century and to build an education system that corresponds. A city that is focused on cultivating talent and deploying it. And most importantly, and relevant to this book, a community keyed in to the notion that America's ability to produce a more talented society will define the success of our nation.

At one point during my visit to Grand Rapids, I inquired about the rapids themselves—the ones along the Grand River for which the city was named. They are long gone, dammed up over a century ago. But a team of local entrepreneurs has recently launched an ambitious plan to restore the rapids. It will take a considerable amount of money and energy, but the project is underway. "It will take years," admits Klohs. She then adds, without missing a beat, "but it will get done!"

After visiting Grand Rapids, I don't doubt her.

So how can other cities "restore the rapids" and make their own talent hubs that will drive economic development, improve quality of life, and make prosperity a reality for larger numbers of people? A few key things come to mind.

One is making clear that place matters. This is not a profound thought, but it is a reality we must insist upon in a world where our lives have become increasingly digital, disparate, and sometimes dehumanized. Prosperity is experienced collectively as much as it is experienced individually—success is often defined by what we share with others. Take sports, for example. Sure, you're happy when your team wins, because it makes you feel good about their accomplishment. But a team's success—and even its failure—is often best experienced when shared with others. Take the 2014 US Men's World Cup soccer team. Its meteoric rise to prominence over the course of a month captured the hearts and minds of millions who had never experienced the joys of futbol before. They didn't win the Cup, but they did win over a lot of fans.

Place is about collaboration—the satisfaction in creating together, and experiencing the fruits of that co-creation as a community. Building more talented and vibrant communities has to be done collaboratively, as we saw in Grand Rapids, among a wide array of people and groups, all working together toward agreed-upon outcomes.

That leads to another key to making cities successful centers of talent development and deployment: goals. The collaborative mindset must be focused, at the beginning, on shared outcomes and an understanding of what needs to be accomplished.

The goal-setting has to be more than just an exercise. It needs to be about translating need into action. A good example is the work that has been done in the past few years in Columbus, Indiana.

This midsize city in southeastern Indiana is, as noted earlier, home to Cummins Inc., one of the world's largest diesel engine manufacturers, as well as some of the most innovative architecture and city planning in the Midwest, and, relevant to the metropolitan revolution, the Columbus Community Education Coalition (CCEC). The latter is a formalized partnership made up of the same type of community cross-section at work in Grand Rapids—business leaders, elected officials, local philanthropists, educators—subordinating their egos and immediate needs to come up with effective methods to match the city's school system to its economic goals.[128]

The CCEC's actions impact and ultimately benefit Columbus children in prekindergarten all the way to young adults on their way to college. The CCEC's bimonthly meetings allow local companies to express what talents and credentials they are looking for in potential and future employees, and educators can then adjust their curriculums going as far back as kindergarten to produce a workforce designed to meet those needs.

An example of the CCEC's work is iGrad, a counseling program focused on dropout prevention in Columbus's high schools. Conceived at a series of CCEC meetings and administered by Ivy Tech Community College and Columbus and Bartholomew County Consolidated School Corp., the program addresses many of the root causes—social and academic—head-on through personal counseling, which is supplied by community volunteers. At one of the city's high schools, East High, forty-four seniors participated in the program, forty-two received their diplomas, and thirty-two went on to college. As a result of this success, Cummins has launched similar programs in Charleston, South Carolina, and in the UK, where the company has other plants. It's another example of a community coming together to help its young people, and as a fortunate byproduct, create a focused and talented workforce that is tailor-made to the needs of local businesses.[129]

Columbus, like Grand Rapids, is a great example of this type of urban progress, but there have to be rewards in place at milestones that encourage people to continue and inspire others to catch on. An effective reward system in the case of cities might be better schools, higher-paying jobs, a renewed sense of cultural connectedness. Talent as it is actualized has to lead to flourishing, to a quality of life and well-being that is measurably and perceptively better than it was before.

What do successful cities do to encourage talent development? They set goals; they listen to what employers need; they foster a sense of place; they offer multiple pathways to success for all types of people; and they work together, harmoniously, driven by the idea that this place—our home—can be restored, with people at the core to ensure that it is even better than it was before. In a sense, they make good on many of the ideas discussed earlier in this book. They take advantage of the educational resources at their disposal, focusing them on what the individual needs to be successful in the community. They use the ingenuity and drive of the private sector, combined with smart public policies, to create a higher level of success. And they recognize that talent comes from many places, including from the outside, in ways that amplify and complement the talent that's already in place. In cities, much like America itself, talent defines what a city is and where it is going.

PART III

TALENT AND AMERICAN PROSPERITY

10

THE SECOND AMERICAN CENTURY

Henry Luce died in the spring of 1967, leaving behind an empire of print journalism that at varying points included *Time*, *Sports Illustrated*, *Fortune*, and many others, and of course a to-be-fulfilled prophecy about America's place in the world. The venue for that prediction, *Life* magazine, closed shop in 2007. *Life*, ironically, was a casualty of the decline of print journalism that, in a way, is a consequence of the dynamism of the past century that redefined how we create and consume media.

So Luce and *Life* are long gone. In their absence, and without any pretensions of being anywhere near their equal in importance and influence, let me try my own hand at prophecy: I believe the 21st century will be the Second American Century.

At first blush, that prediction seems to run contrary to many visible signs.

In the autumn of 2014, Politico published a poll revealing that 64 percent of Americans felt that their country was "out of control."[130] One could almost string together an entire essay of the polls and surveys taken since the Great Recession that demonstrate the current jittery American mindset. But similar studies would have indicated the same thing during Luce's time, as America struggled to exit the Great Depression while war and tyranny engulfed Europe.

Today we are seeing a mixed bag of signs of economic life after the economic downturn that has defined this era, and wars (both declared and undeclared) still rage across the globe. But while World War II triggered the first American Century, a similar cataclysm is not likely in the cards today. No rational person would wish for that.

Alternatively, we have no other choice but to focus our attention on what our society needs in order to usher in another eight decades of rising prosperity and societal flourishing. We need to think clearly about the benefits of a more talented society and what it means for America's future. And then we must act.

My battle plan, those all-important five ways, is to create a more talented society by:

- *rethinking the enterprise of higher education* to focus tightly on the students themselves and on the learning outcomes that will impact economic and social progress;

- *unleashing private sector innovation* to apply the risk-taking capacities of philanthropy, business, and capital markets to solve the talent deficit;

- *repurposing three different federal agencies* into a new US Department of Talent that would put talent at the center of federal workforce, education, and recruitment policies;

- *developing a new immigration model* that applies the lessons of successful models like Australia's so that we use immigration as a talent enhancement strategy for the nation; and

- *recognizing metropolitan areas* not as problems for the nation to solve, but as hubs of talent where innovation and commerce thrive and increase the nation's human potential.

Here's the thing, though. I can say "do these five things, and PRESTO, we will have another era of peace and prosperity!" That's too easy. The question, apart from the platitudes, is what can the United States expect in terms of the benefits that result from the successful implementation of these five ideas? If the changes suggested in this book actually happen—if policy is changed, if collaboration improves, if more talent is made or imported—what does the country receive in return? What, specifically, does American society look like if we achieve this higher level of talent? What will the Second American Century have in store?

The answer comes in two parts. One can be related in data and research, the other through our imaginations.

Let's start with the first category.

I discussed the talent imperative with John Engler, the former governor of Michigan whom we heard from earlier. Engler, a popular three-term chief executive of the Great Lake State and former CEO of the National Association of Manufacturers, is now president of the Business Roundtable, the most influential association of CEOs of leading companies in the United States, and perhaps the world. "A society is an aggregation of all these individuals; it's the Gross Education Product of the USA," he argued, coining a useful new metric. "It's how we sum up all of these investments we have made for individuals and what they have done for them as people and us as a nation."

He added: "This is the most significant investment we make. If your GEP rises, so does your GDP. It's a measurable relationship."

It's a great concept, the GEP. And Governor Engler generously offered it up for this book with no interest in credit for its creation. That was an offer I had to refuse. But I will happily borrow the GEP concept and refashion it into a gauge to measure what a more talented America, the key to another American Century, will look like. In other words, a Gross *Talent* Product, or GTP.

First, we need to define the numbers or core facts that describe what a more talented society looks like. What exactly would our Gross Talent Product be? If we can determine that, we've got a fairly conservative estimate of what prosperity looks like. After all, we know that talent also comes from immigration, from the collaborative capacities of cities, and from other sources. So the Gross Talent Product is a sort of floor for the discussion about how talent ultimately impacts prosperity.

The only way to look to the future is to look at where we are now. That requires unpacking and sifting through some academic research and statistics. But it's important to understand that the idea that we can describe and, to a certain degree, actually measure the impact of talent on prosperity isn't wishful thinking—it's based on clear evidence.

The demand for talent is large and growing. Economists at the Georgetown University Center on Education and the Workforce found, for example, that since 1983, the demand for college-educated workers has grown by an average rate of 3 percent each year, while the supply has only grown by 2 percent.[131] That's why the earnings advantage of a college degree over a high school degree jumped from 39 percent to 84 percent since the early eighties, as employers competed for new college talent.[132]

What's behind these changes? Most economists believe that advances in technology have improved productivity and thus reduced the demand for manufacturing workers. Meanwhile, the growing importance of technology in the overall economy has increased the demand for educated workers who can utilize it. This increasing demand for highly educated workers has been the defining feature of our postindustrial economy.

Moreover, in today's economy, plain vanilla is no longer good enough. Variety and the customization of goods and services have become key competitive principles.[133] New cars now come with interactive guidance systems, onboard computers, rearview and side cameras, and a dizzying array of other options, and the old world of three TV networks has been replaced with thousands of cable channels and Internet-only programs and news sources. Increasingly, consumers have neither the time nor patience for shoddy goods or second-rate services.

As consumer taste and preferences became more sophisticated, firms and workers required more talent to compete. Companies demand a deeper and broader set of skills from their workers: not just cognitive skills, but interpersonal skills and other noncognitive competencies. Employers have raised entry-level educational requirements for their workers and expect them to engage in lifelong learning on the job.

Producing today's high-quality goods and services requires employees to have a deeper knowledge of their fields of study and a better understanding of applications on the job. Growing demands for variety and customization require the flexibility to master short production runs and various consumer interactions. Greater expectations of convenience, customer service, and social responsibility require empathy for the customer or client. The endless quest for innovation requires deep domain knowledge, critical thinking skills, creativity, and a tolerance for change.

Modern information technology is ultimately biased in favor of highly skilled workers because it supplements more than it substitutes for skill. In the workplace, information technology is both a substitute and a complement to human skill. Right now it's less like the Jetsons and more like what we might ·

have expected when computers were first introduced. Computer technology automates repetitive tasks but leaves nonrepetitive tasks and higher levels of human interaction to workers who in turn require higher levels of cognitive and noncognitive competencies. Virtually all workers now have nonroutine interactions with more powerful and flexible technology. Computers have become more like an artisan's tool, reflecting complex human input, and less like the single-purpose mass-production machines characteristic of the industrial economy.

Today, for every task surrendered to automation, new opportunities are generated for exploiting the technology's capabilities. Moreover, the more flexible and powerful the machinery, the more employees, work teams, and organizations must increase their skills to fully deploy its technical capabilities. These more flexible and powerful technologies work best in combination with more flexible and highly skilled workers to deliver quality, variety, customization, convenience, brand consistency, speed, and innovation at the lowest cost.

As the demand for postsecondary education and training has increased, high school graduates have been left behind. Wage data tell this story with startling clarity. Between 1970 and 2010, high school–educated men's wages declined by 41 percent as young men lost access to middle-wage, blue-collar jobs in the manufacturing industry and have been forced to shift into lower-paying food, personal service, sales, and office support occupations.[134]

Let's return to the discussion about knowledge, skills, and abilities mentioned earlier. The impact of the distinct talents, general skills, and competencies on a nation's workforce is one important way to understand what happens when you have more talent at a societal level. For example, data on wages and salaries tell us that employers are increasingly paying higher wages for certain types of skills. In other words, the economy is creating more jobs and paying higher wages for skills that require workers to solve complex problems and think critically. Since educational attainment and occupational choice are directly related to wages, we can actually isolate the impact of remaining competencies in the same manner.

The result is about what you'd expect. Though we know that jobs in the STEM fields—Science, Technology, Engineering, and Math—and managerial occupations tend to pay relatively higher wages than many others, highly educated managerial, STEM, and healthcare professional workers get the greatest monetary return for relatively higher levels of problem-solving skills. There are marginal benefits to problem-solving skills within occupations that are positively related to education level. The same argument is true for critical thinking. Relatively higher levels of critical thinking skills are rewarded at their highest levels to holders of a bachelor's degree and above, regardless of occupation.

Figure 8. Share of Value Added by Education, 1980–2012

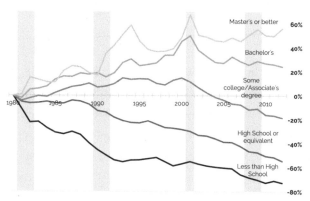

Source: *Georgetown University Center on Education and the Workforce analysis of O*NET 17.0 and ACS 2011*

Figure 9. Median Earnings Increase with Educational Attainment and Level of Complex Problem Solving

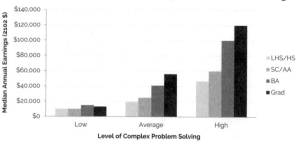

Source: *Georgetown University Center on Education and the Workforce analysis of O*NET 17.0 and ACS 2011*

Figure 10. Median Earnings Increase with Educational Attainment and Level of Critical Thinking Skills

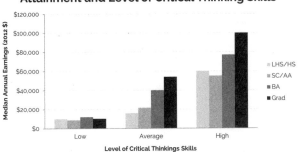

Source: *Georgetown University Center on Education and the Workforce analysis of O*NET 17.0 and ACS 2011*

But in spite of all these trends, the talent supply isn't keeping up with demand. Our failure to produce enough college talent results in economic output below potential and leads to growing income inequality. That failure to produce enough college talent costs us $500 billion in lost Gross Domestic Product, the monetary value of all goods and services produced in a country, which would generate at least another $110 billion in tax revenue, according to Tony Carnevale, who leads the Georgetown University Center on Education and the Workforce.[135]

Among high school students, college-age young adults, and older adults, the United States lags substantially behind its peers in literacy, numeracy, and problem solving in technology-rich environments. US teenagers and high school graduates have weaker basic skills than their international peers—especially in math, where 25 percent score below the baseline level, compared to 10 percent in Finland and Korea.[136] What's more, they don't seem to be catching up: Between 1994 and 2004, there was no growth in US teenagers' literacy skills. Baby boomers rank average in numeracy skills relative to their international peers, and American teenagers and college-age adults rank dead last in numeracy.[137]

In terms of postsecondary attainment, the United States is actually losing ground to its international peers. The baby boom generation ranks first in bachelor's degree attainment and third in postsecondary attainment internationally, but as discussed earlier, today's generation of young adults is not faring as well, standing at a depressing twelfth in bachelor's degree attainment and eleventh in postsecondary attainment overall. The largest room for growth is in career-focused associate degree programs, where the United States ranks seventeenth internationally, at 10 percent. By comparison, 25 percent of young adults in Canada earn a career-focused associate degree.[138]

Under current projections, the US will need eleven million more workers with postsecondary credentials between 2014 and 2020 to satisfy the labor market's demand for college-educated workers. The recession of 2007–09 led to the decline of low-skill construction and manufacturing jobs; what took their place were jobs in healthcare, biotech, nanotech, clean energy, and advanced manufacturing, most of which require at least an associate degree. This increased the level of skills mismatch in the labor market, as former construction and manufacturing workers scrambled to retrain and move into different careers.

Prosperity resulting from the educational impact on talent can be measured in another way. A more talented society would also result in a more equal society. That's because a huge part of what's driving growing inequality is the college wage premium—the difference in earnings between high school graduates and college graduates. While much of the focus of the public inequality discussion has been on the top 1 percent versus the 99 percent, the single most important factor that determines inequality among the 99 percent is the growing returns of a college degree.

The economist David Autor provides an illuminating example of this fact. If you look at growing inequality between 1979 and 2012, and divide the gains of the 1 percent among the 99 percent, each family would get $7,000. If you took the gains of college-educated families over the same time period and divided them up among the high school–educated families, each family would get $28,000![139]

So the academic research and statistics make a clear-cut case for investing more in talent creation. Let's be clear, though: The benefits of a more talented society, the components, if you will, of prosperity, aren't entirely captured by economic statistics. The dollars-and-cents benefits of creating this more talented society are pretty straightforward. But they don't capture all the benefits. That's because unmeasured increases in the material quality of life—including increases in things like quality, variety, customization, convenience, and more information—are beyond the reach of economic statistics.

The standard metric economists use to measure growth is productivity or GDP per worker. But these statistics don't capture these obvious improvements in the standard of living, because the stuff we consume today is just different than what we consumed 100 years ago. The economist Brad Delong has a great example illustrating this point in his essay "How Fast Is Modern Economic Growth?" If you take away all the gains from productivity growth since 1867, the average American would earn $7,500 per year.[140] But today's average American making $7,500 per year is clearly much better off because she can use some of that money to buy antibiotics, a stove, or a television set—something Americans in 1867 just couldn't do.

Or consider that you can now put what was once known as a supercomputer in your pocket. But how effectively you are able to use that supercomputer depends on *talent*, or how effectively your knowledge, skills, and abilities complement the technologies of the modern day.

Figuring out how to express this in financial terms is challenging, in part because you get to some numbers that are hard to fathom. In the world we live in today, big numbers don't shock as much as they used to. But solid, conservative analysis still should help us understand the total impact of education outcomes on our national well-being, measured in dollar terms. The problem is, we become almost numb to the size of the numbers. For example, a recent analysis showed that an investment of $310 billion more in education today would yield a benefit of $225 trillion over an eighty-year period—essentially the lifespan of an entire generation of workers.[141] Sounds impressive, but honestly, it's such a fantastical number, laden with assumptions, that it's hard to know what to do with it.

Adding to the complexity is that, while we've gotten pretty good at measuring activity that occurs inside markets, we don't measure as well activity that occurs outside of those confines. Yet the out-of-market benefits you get from talent are just as real.

Several researchers have taken the challenge on by attempting to dig deeper into this question of market versus nonmarket benefits. And this is where it gets interesting. One of the most important analyses of these nonmarket benefits was conducted by Michael Christian in 2011. He found that those nonmarket benefits from higher levels of talent come to between half as much to the same as the market benefits of higher wages and employment. In monetary terms, the value of education investment is $7 trillion: $3.7 trillion of market value and $3.3 trillion of nonmarket value.[142] But because we don't measure the nonmarket value, we don't factor it into our public and private investment decisions. As a result, we've been significantly underinvesting in talent.

In essence, this combination of both market and nonmarket value is the idea that Governor Engler and I talked about—a Gross Talent Product, a way to express the impact of increasing talent on prosperity. Investing in talent produces $7 trillion of market and nonmarket value each year. Think about what that really means. That's more value than the economies of Brazil, India, and the United Kingdom produce each year—combined.

Talent is more than a set of ideas, wrapped in conceptual frameworks. Investing in the Five Ways to attract, educate, and deploy talent will result in outcomes that are real. At least some of those outcomes, particularly the ones based on education, are measurable, including the market and nonmarket value discussed here. Talent is the key to our future growth—economically, culturally, socially. Americans can gain much greater levels of prosperity from investing in talent development and deployment. But they also will pay a much higher price than they do today if we don't realize the benefits that higher talent offers.

"When I was governor, I always believed that the state with the best talent wins," John Engler told me. "But it has become true today that the nation with the best talent is likely to win."

To Engler's point, the GTP is an expression of the total impact that investment in education, immigration, and other systems and processes have on the nation. A higher GTP means more talent for the nation, and more talent leads to amazing impacts on the prosperity of the American people. It's a simple but powerful way to describe why America needs talent, more than ever before.

Now that we can better understand the real, measurable impact of a more talented society, we can better imagine what that society will look like in the future. This is clearly getting into the realm of prognostication and speculation, but it's also derived from the evidence base we've just worked through.

For starters, the Second American Century will be a much more equitable one, where employers see how much value is added to their businesses from having more diverse employee populations, and where policy makers recognize that the talent derived from broad-based immigration policies, education strategies, and social innovation efforts leads to a wide level of prosperity for all Americans.

The prosperity of the country will no longer be driven by the size of our economy, reputations of our education institutions, or the decaying nature of our cities. It will be replaced by an outlook where a nimble approach to talent development and deployment meets the growing thirst for variety and customization that define our work lives and our personal interests. In this new century, the innovation of the private sector will be aimed increasingly at meeting America's social as well as economic objectives, creating ever more opportunities for self-renewal and growth.

In the Second American Century, a talent-focused federal agency infrastructure will more nimbly anticipate talent needs for the country. That capacity to plan ahead will allow federal investments to be more sharply focused on increasing talent levels in our rapidly changing economy as needs emerge.

For example, a talent shortage in an area like artificial intelligence (AI)—which is currently dominated mostly by military defense contractors and government intelligence agencies, but which could rapidly emerge as a field with broad societal implications—could be addressed by coordinated federal strategies. A US Department of Talent could aim its education investment strategies specifically at the AI field, giving preference to postsecondary programs of study to meet rising student-driven demand for this type of education. The department's education-focused work could be linked to its training efforts, so that incumbent workers in certain fields could be retrained directly by employers, or by other providers. And a talent-weighted immigration policy managed by the department could be tipped in favor of individuals who come from the best AI apprentice programs around the world.

If we had a more talented, more diverse, and better-trained and better-educated populace in the coming decades, think of what that could produce and how it would impact the well-being, not just of Americans, but of people all across the world.

Henry Luce called the 20th century a "revolutionary" epoch. Revolutionary in science and industry, and societal structure, he wrote. And indeed it was. But the 21st century holds the potential to be even more so. If, for just a moment, we give free rein to our imaginations, we can glimpse the possibilities. They are remarkable.

American engineers can guarantee that we are the first to set foot on the surface of Mars. But hey, why stop at the Red Planet? We could also be the first to colonize the moon, or at least begin to put the pieces in place to do so.

American scientists and doctors can discover cures for AIDS, cancer, Alzheimer's, and ALS. And we can quickly respond to and eradicate emerging dangers such as Ebola, SARS, and other deadly diseases.

American innovators can create the next digital devices that change the way we live and work. Personal computers, cellphones, iPhones… these are already in the rearview window in the Second American Century. The large-scale implementation of self-driving vehicles, wearable and biometric technology, and powerful new tools that redefine how we work can all blossom and grow in America.

A renaissance in American music, film, literature, and all of the other forms of our cultural currency can not only continue to be the world's most vital, but also be the most influential, even in this time of great globalization.

Along the way, our schools, universities, libraries and other centers of learning can be the best in the world, our workforce the most skilled. The talent we develop and deploy can be recognized for its excellence around the world, with demand increasing for the opportunity to live and work in a nation where knowledge, skills, and abilities return so much to individuals and society.

All of these things will bring with them great prosperity. Prosperous nations are compassionate nations. So in this Second American Century, we will reduce income disparity and level poverty. A wealthy society is also one that can and will honor its commitments, those made to our most vulnerable and those made to our creditors.

Too rosy of a scenario? I honestly don't believe so. With a more talented society, it's within our grasp.

CONCLUSION

If you're an avid television watcher, the title of this book may conjure the name of a successful reality-based show, *America's Got Talent*. On the show, an echo of the classic talent/variety show from the sixties and seventies, a cavalcade of dancers, singers, comedians, and the like are pitted in a competition that ultimately results in a million-dollar prize for the winner. The show is perfectly enjoyable if not predictable, but it's not really the kind of talent that will make our nation stronger and more vibrant. As we've discussed, the term "talent" is much more than that; its frequent misuse probably clouds our understanding of why it is so important to American society.

Here's another example: In the final weeks of America's 2014 midterm elections, Bloomberg.com aired a vignette also titled "America's Got Talent."[143] This three-minute clip was merely a discussion on the merits of some commercials that potential 2016 presidential candidates had made for their campaigns or to aid fellow office seekers. That's it.

So "talent" is applied in many different contexts, and is a concept that might confuse many more than it enlightens. Still, the show, the commercials, and all of the other ways in which we tend to invoke the concept of "talent" demonstrate that we respond in visceral ways to the idea that talent is something we inherently possess as Americans; it is at the core of our national persona. If nothing else, the confluence of the term "talent" in those commercials and our next presidential election—the time when we most often talk as a nation about what it means to be American—is fortuitous.

This is not a political book. It doesn't support any political party or doctrine, but it does, I hope, have something that legislators, thought leaders, and office seekers, not to mention business leaders and civic organizations, can glean and put to use in the coming years. The ideas presented here cut across the typical lines of ideology, professional perspective, or geography. Talent has no interest group; its benefits are shared by all Americans.

And I have some circumstantial evidence to back up this view that getting to a more talented society is a shared American value. During the year or so of writing *America Needs Talent*, I met with an incredibly diverse cast of characters: CEOs of investment firms and Fortune 500 companies, higher educators and government officials; innovators of all types; Democrats, Republicans, and everything in between. Some were interviews for this book, some were at dinner parties and social events, and still others were tied to my speaking engagements at forums like the Aspen Ideas Festival.

In almost every case, the conversation started out in the same manner: I shared with them the impetus behind the book—the concern about the future of the country and its correlation to the talent gap. To a person, and without prodding, their thoughts inevitably arrived at the same conclusion: Our country is in trouble, we are facing deficits of prosperity and opportunity, in danger of losing our global standing as a leader, both economically and culturally, and we are on track to leaving a less-influential and less-prosperous country to our children and grandchildren.

But this sentiment was often followed quickly by the shared faith that a solution, the way to check this downward drift, was not at all out of reach; that cultivating a new generation of thinkers, makers, risk takers, and impresarios is the key, and the talent needed to do so is at our fingertips.

Not everyone agreed on how we should do it or what policies would accomplish it, but the consensus was clear: America needs talent.

I set out to collect, synthesize, and adapt various innovative thoughts, notions, and suggestions while hopefully dropping a few original ideas into the stew as well. Here's what I concluded.

Our higher education system is dysfunctional, costly, and largely unaccountable for its actual purpose (preparing Americans for productive careers and engaged lives). As a result, skepticism is surrounding the value of a college degree at a time when our economy, now more than ever, demands workers with skills only found in postsecondary learning environments. Let's redesign higher education as we know it, make it both affordable and accessible, bring it into the 21st century, add much more transparency to the system, and redefine how we credential students and measure their learning outcomes. Learning is the key to the success of the higher education system, and the learning that students obtain should be the most important thing we measure—not how much time they spent in a classroom, and not which school they attended.

The public sector has its role to play in addressing our societal concerns and developing and training talent. So, too, does the philanthropic world. But what if they were joined by a powerful partner? Let private markets, with their assets, resources, and know-how, be the difference maker. They can play a role in guiding and financing education for employees and potential employees, and advancing human outcomes. New forms of public-private partnerships, like social innovation bonds, are pointing toward a new compact between those who manage or generate financial capital and those who seek social return. These efforts at encouraging private sector innovation could yield enormous benefits for our talent infrastructure in the coming years.

The federal government is full of well-intentioned programs, a number of which have worked spectacularly. Others have made some progress, and still others have simply not worked. Like so many areas, our government is in the talent development business, and the final product is less than desirable. Let's consolidate and improve these programs, often charged with redundant and even at times conflicting missions and spread out across numerous agencies, into one streamlined federal department dedicated to training and deploying American talent. A US Department of Talent would not be an addition to the existing array of federal bureaucratic institutions, but instead would draw together the atomized functions in three different entities—the Education Department, parts of the Labor Department, and the talent recruitment functions currently buried in the Department of Homeland Security.

America, that land of immigrants, the world's beacon of hope and opportunity, has naturalization laws so byzantine and counterintuitive that brilliant minds, men and women who could be our next Steve Jobs or Jonas Salk, would often rather leave our shores, PhDs in hand, than navigate our immigration system. In some cases they are not coming here at all. Let's stop the endless political Kabuki routine and create a new immigration system, one built around what type of talent we need to create the society we want to live in. That talent recruitment can't just focus on the high end, however. It must recognize that talent comes in many forms, and all of them should count in building our collective base of knowledge, skills, and abilities. And let's not be shy about looking abroad for inspiration on how to do so. Australia has made major progress in this area, and we can learn from their experiences while applying the lessons in ways that reflect our unique economic and cultural fabric.

Our media outlets seem to regularly print stories on the sad and scary plight of American cities. Bankrupt, dangerous, dysfunctional. But what if a crop of urban areas, thanks to smart leadership, civic-minded businesses, and engaged citizens turned their homes into hubs of innovation and commerce? This one's not a hypothetical. It's actually happening, away from the headlines, in places like Grand Rapids, Michigan, and Columbus, Indiana. Let's encourage more of our cities to follow suit, and talent will find a new seedbed.

Taken together, these Five Ways to attract, educate, and deploy talent will ensure our prosperity as a nation. They will, in the best case, present a blueprint. One that will create a more talented society, and as a result, a prosperous one—a Second American Century that can be envisioned in facts and numbers, and in our imaginations. Worst case, they take a subject on many minds, conversations many are having, a notion many are accepting, with some resignation, and place it firmly in the public discourse. I have no stake in the 2016 presidential election, nor does the foundation I lead, at least not in the partisan sense. But we, like all Americans, have much riding on the coming years, when policy makers, thought leaders, and business executives must right this nation for the remainder of the 21st century.

The path to get us there is surely quite different than the one we followed in the 20th century. But the inspiration for this renewal may be the same one that motivated Henry Luce when he spoke of the first American Century back in 1941:

> Other nations can survive simply because they have endured so long—sometimes with more and sometimes with less significance. But this nation, conceived in adventure

and dedicated to the progress of man—this nation cannot truly endure unless there courses strongly through its veins from Maine to California the blood of purposes and enterprise and high resolve.

The 21st century prosperity of this country, its cultural standing, its role as a world leader, its workforce, these things are all in doubt.[144] The American people are perceptive. And they sense all of this. They are also, by the way, resourceful, hardworking, diverse, intelligent, and still blessed to live in the freest nation in the world. They still have within them the ability to cure disease, to explore the cosmos, to invent the next indispensable device that changes the world. The raw material is still here. But the clock is running and the time to develop and redeploy it is at hand. The fate of our future is riding on getting this right. And I have every faith that we will do exactly that.

ACKNOWLEDGMENTS

It turns out that writing a book is humbling—it's a pretty hard thing to do. Writing a book while serving as the head of a large national foundation might be seen by some as bordering on foolish. I was fortunate in the year that I spent working on this book to have the amazing support and contributions of many people who made that hard work easier, and who ensured that my ambition did not make me look nearly as foolish as I feared when I set out to work on this project.

I owe my greatest thanks to Ryan Cole, who served as thought partner and confidant throughout this project. Though Ryan and I had not worked closely together before I set out to write the book, he developed an uncanny ability to understand where I was coming from and offered an array of meaningful contributions, from research support to effective prose to some wonderful historical references.

My colleagues at Lumina Foundation deserve credit for making this book much better, thanks to their close reading, feedback, and unflagging enthusiasm. Kiko Suarez, who expertly cajoled me into writing this book and was personally encouraging and supportive throughout the process, was the wind in the sails of the Lumina support effort, with Holly McKiernan, Dewayne Matthews, Danette Howard, Sam Cargile, Dave Maas, Sean Tierney, and Stefanie Krevda providing great counsel and ideas that sharpened the message and reduced the muddied thinking and inexact prose that inevitably emerge when writing something of this length. Lucia Weathers and Kirsten Cuniffe did a marvelous job of helping to frame the message and to push the ideas out well beyond Lumina's current audiences.

I am grateful to the board of directors at Lumina Foundation, which responded enthusiastically to my idea of writing the book, even though they understood that it would discuss issues and ideas that go well beyond the purview of the foundation's mission. Individually and collectively, Lumina's board members have been a source of inspiration for this work, because they have consistently pressed me to take our work in postsecondary learning and apply it to the broader needs of society and the country. Not all CEOs can say what I have said unabashedly throughout my tenure at Lumina Foundation: I have a great board, and I'm privileged to do this job with the support and encouragement of such a committed group of board colleagues.

I was honored to have the critical feedback of three trusted external colleagues who provided data and information and offered critical feedback on a prior draft of the book. Heartfelt thanks go to Tony Carnevale at the Georgetown Center on Education and the Workforce, whose high-quality work is reflected throughout this book, including in many of the original data analyses highlighted in the text and graphics; Bruce Katz, the guru of metropolitan studies at the Brookings Institution; and Thomas Parker, my long-time friend, colleague, and straight-talking mentor.

Several people are quoted in this book, individuals who were willing to take the time to talk through my ideas about the talent paradigm for the country. Those conversations have made the ideas contained here stronger, clearer, and hopefully more concrete. Thanks to Sangeeta Bharadwaj-Badal; Jim Clifton; Mohamed El-Erian; John Engler; Martha Kanter; Tom Linebarger; Blair Taylor; and Nancy Zimpher.

I am indebted to Birgit Klohs, the president and CEO of Grand Rapids' The Right Place, for making it possible for me to see the metropolitan revolution up close and in person. Thanks also to the following people for generously giving their time and offering their insights during my visit to Grand Rapids: Rick Chapla, Steve Ender, Bing Goei, Mayor George Heartwell, John Helmholdt, Mary Jo Kuhiman, Kevin McCurren, Michael Ramirez, Lynne Robinson, Kelly Savage, Diana Sieger, Kevin Stotts, Michelle VanDyke, and Miles Wilson.

Janette Haughton, Minister Counselor for Immigration at the Embassy of Australia in Washington, generously chatted about and shed light on her country's immigration policies, for which I am grateful. Mark Cully, the former chief economist for the Australian Department of Immigration and Citizenship, was a terrific guide as well. And Tamar Jacoby, an outstanding American analyst who has written widely about the challenges the US faces in its immigration policies, provided sage counsel and access to information and resources regarding several of the ideas about immigration that I attempt to explore in this book.

Thanks to our partners at Vox Global for their input and ideas throughout this process. Mike Marker and the team at Vox Global have been terrific allies over the course of many years and have encouraged me to elevate my voice on the national stage more regularly.

Deep appreciation to my editor Merrill Perlman, who is an admirable combination of thorough, insightful, and quick. Merrill's careful work has helped me turn my ideas and musings into a published product that I hope is worthy of the energy she has put into it.

I began the *America Needs Talent* journey back in 2013 and wasn't even sure I was ready to write the book at all. But a meeting with Arthur Klebanoff, agent extraordinaire and publishing world innovator, motivated me to take the time to express my ideas about talent in this form. He and his colleagues at the Scott Meredith Literary Agency and RosettaBooks have been enthusiasts and realists—two traits that probably strike the right balance when you are trying to influence national thinking about such an expansive area of public interest. Thanks to the RosettaBooks team for effortlessly shepherding this book to publication, especially Hannah Bennett, Peter Clark, Navjot Khalsa, Brehanna Ramirez, and Michelle Weyenberg.

Finally, I can't adequately describe how much I appreciate the support and love I have received from my wonderful wife, Colleen O'Brien, and our endlessly curious children, Benjamin and Elizabeth. Colleen has played many roles in our life partnership, among them spouse, mother, business partner, editor, and best friend. Her passion for equity, her obsession with sports, her insightful ideas and intellectual prodding, all have shaped who I am and what I care most about. This book couldn't have happened without her.

NOTES

1. THE AMERICAN CENTURY

1. Henry Luce, "The American Century," *Life*, February 17, 1941.

2. Arthur Herman, *Freedom's Forge, How American Business Produced Victory in World War II*, Random House, 2013.

3. David M. Oshinsky, *Polio: An American Story*, Oxford University Press, 2005.

4. "Vaccines Have Beaten Back Global Diseases Such as Smallpox and Polio," *The Washington Post*, April 11, 2011.

5. Dennis Thompson, "The Salk Polio Vaccine: 'Greatest Public Health Experiment in History,'" CBS News, December 2, 2014.

6. "Sputnik Spurs Passage of National Defense Education Act," Senate.gov.

7. John F. Kennedy Address at Rice University, September 12, 1962.

8. "150th Anniversary of the Land-Grant College Act," Rutgers.edu.

9. James B. Hunt Jr., "Educational Leadership for the 21st Century," HigherEducation.org.

10. "The G.I. Bill: Paving the Way to a Better America," Grantham University.

11. The Higher Education Act of 1965, P.L. 89-329.

12. The Immigration Act of 1924 (The Johnson-Reed Act).

2. A NATION AT RISK

13. "Bush Unveils Vision for Moon and Beyond," CNN.com, January 15, 2004.

14. John F. Harris and John E. Yang, "Clinton to Sign Bill Overhauling Welfare," *The Washington Post*, August 1, 1996.

15. Christopher Graff, "Jeffords Leaves Republican Party," *The Washington Post*, May 24, 2001.

16. Jim Jeffords, *My Declaration of Independence*, Simon & Schuster, 2001.

17. "Panel Urges College Aid Overhaul," *The Washington Post*, February 3, 1993.

18. "Bush Space Plan Faces Opposition," CNN.com, January 14, 2004.

19. Amrutha Gayathri, "US 17th In Global Education Rankings," *International Business Times,* November 27, 2012.

20. "US Students Still Lag Behind Foreign Peers," The Huffington Post, July 23, 2012.

21. Anthony P. Carnevale, Nicole Smith, and Jeff Strohl, "Recovery: Job Growth and Education Requirements Through 2020," Georgetown University Center on Education and the Workforce, June 2013.

22. OECD (2014), *Education at a Glance 2014: OECD Indicators,* OECD Publishing.

23. Anthony P. Carnevale and Nicole Smith, "America's Future Workforce," in *All-In Nation: An America that Works for All,* Center for American Progress, 2013.

24. "How Is the Global Talent Pool Changing?" Organization for Economic Cooperation and Development, May 2012.

25. Elise Young, "Global Education Shifts," *Inside Higher Ed,* July 12. 2012.

26. "President Obama Announces Move to Overhaul Immigration," *The Wall Street Journal,* November 20, 2014.

27. Sheldon G. Adelson, Warren E. Buffett, and Bill Gates, "Break the Immigration Impasse," *The New York Times,* July 11, 2014.

28. "Senate Kills Bush Immigration Bill," Reuters, June 29, 2007.

29. Nick Leiber, "At Spain's Door, a Welcome Mat for Entrepreneurs," *The New York Times,* November 22, 2014.

30. Steve Case, "As Congress Dawdles, The World Steals Our Talent," *The Wall Street Journal,* September 9, 2013.

31. "Immigration and the Revival of American Cities," Americas Society/Council of the Americas, September 2013.

32. Ron Fournier and Sophie Quinton, "In Nothing We Trust," *National Journal,* April 21, 2012.

33. Megan O'Neil, "Americans' Engagement With Organizations Wanes, Report Says," *The Chronicle of Philanthropy,* December 12, 2014.

34. "Midterm Elections 2014 Exit Polls," *The Wall Street Journal,* November 5, 2014.

35. Brendan Bordelon, "European Space Head Gloats over 'Best Expertise in the World' after Comet Landing," *National Review,* November 12, 2014.

3. WINNING THE FUTURE

36. Kenneth Rapoza, "By the Time Obama Leaves Office, U.S. No Longer No. 1," *Forbes,* March 23, 2013.

37. Brett Arends, "It's Official: America Is Now No. 2," MarketWatch, December 4, 2014.

38. Clarence Tsui, "Beijing International Screenwriting Competition Announces Winners," *The Hollywood Reporter*, May 21, 2013.

39. Pam Fessler, "How Many Americans Live in Poverty?" NPR, November 6, 2013.

40. Neil Irwin, "The Typical American Family Makes Less Than It Did in 1989," *The Washington Post*, September 17, 2013.

41. Anthony P. Carnevale, Andrew R. Hanson, and Artem Gulish, "Failure to Launch: Structural Shift and the New Lost Generation," Georgetown University Center on Education and the Workforce, September 2013.

42. Anthony P. Carnevale, Andrew R. Hanson, and Artem Gulish, "Failure to Launch: Structural Shift and the New Lost Generation," Georgetown University Center on Education and the Workforce, September 2013.

43. Anthony P. Carnevale, Andrew R. Hanson, and Artem Gulish, "Failure to Launch: Structural Shift and the New Lost Generation," Georgetown University Center on Education and the Workforce, September 2013.

44. Anthony P. Carnevale, Andrew R. Hanson, and Artem Gulish, "Failure to Launch: Structural Shift and the New Lost Generation," Georgetown University Center on Education and the Workforce, September 2013.

45. Anthony P. Carnevale, Andrew R. Hanson, and Artem Gulish, "Failure to Launch: Structural Shift and the New Lost Generation," Georgetown University Center on Education and the Workforce, September 2013.

46. Anthony P. Carnevale, Andrew R. Hanson, and Artem Gulish, "Failure to Launch: Structural Shift and the New Lost Generation," Georgetown University Center on Education and the Workforce, September 2013.

47. "2014 Annual Report of the Boards of Trustees of the Federal Hospital Insurance and Federal Supplementary Medical Insurance Trust Funds," Centers for Medicare & Medicaid Services, July 28, 2014.

48. "Policy Basics: Non-Defense Discretionary Programs," Center on Budget and Policy Priorities, updated April 30, 2014.

4. TALENT, YOU SAY?

49. "Jimi Hendrix: Hear My Train A Comin'," PBS documentary, November 2013.

50. "CEO Route to the Top," Spencer Stuart, May 2013.

51. Eric Turkheimer, Andreana Haley, Mary Waldron, Brian D'Onofrio, and Irving I. Gottesman, "Socioeconomic Status Modifies Heritability of IQ in Young Children," *Psychological Science*, Vol. 14, No. 6, November 2003

52. Sheldon Danziger, Timothy Smeeding, and Lee Rainwater, "The Western Welfare State in the 1990s: Toward a New Model of Antipoverty Policy for Families With Children," Luxembourg Income Study Working Paper No. 128, August 1995.

53. "Child Well-Being in Rich Countries: A Comparative Overview," Innocenti Report Card 11, UNICEF Office of Research, April 2013.

5. IT'S THE LEARNING, STUPID

54. Amanda Ripley, "College Is Dead. Long Live College!" *Time*, October 18, 2012.

55. Charles Murray, "For Most People, College Is a Waste of Time," *The Wall Street Journal*, August 13, 2008.

56. Lauren Weber, "Do Too Many People Go to College?" *The Wall Street Journal*, June 21, 2012.

57. Seth Roberts, "Why College Is Usually a Waste of Time," The Huffington Post, May 25, 2011.

58. "The Big Education Racket," *The Rush Limbaugh Show*, October 27, 2011.

59. "Billionaire Offers College Alternative," CBS News, May 17, 2012.

60. Richard B. Freeman, *The Overeducated American*, Academic Press, 1976.

61. Steve Kolowich, "The MOOC Hype Fades, in 3 Charts," *The Chronicle of Higher Education*, February 5, 2015.

62. William G. Bowen, Matthew M. Chingos, Kelly A. Lack, and Thomas I. Nygren, "Interactive Learning Online at Public Universities: Evidence from Randomized Trials," ITHAKA, May 2012.

63. "Time Is the Enemy: The Surprising Truth About Why Today's College Students Aren't Graduating... and What Needs to Change," Complete College America, September 2011.

64. Kevin Carey, *The End of College: Creating the Future of Learning and the University of Everywhere*, Riverhead Books, 2015.

65. Paul Fain, "Hour by Hour," *Inside Higher Ed*, September 5, 2012.

66. "What Americans Need to Know About Higher Education Redesign." Lumina Gallup Poll, February 25, 2014.

67. "Great Jobs, Great Lives: The 2014 Gallup-Purdue Index Report."

68. Anthony P. Carnevale, Andrew R. Hanson, and Artem Gulish, "Failure to Launch: Structural Shift and the New Lost Generation," Georgetown Center on Education and the Workforce, September 2013.

69. Amy Laitinen, "Cracking the Credit Hour," New America Foundation and Education Sector, September 2012.

70. "Associate Accelerated Program (ASAP)," Ivy Tech Community College, accessed April 24, 2015.

71. Paul Fain, "Competency and Affordability," *Inside Higher Ed*, May 6, 2014.

72. Paul J. LeBlanc, "Accreditation in a Rapidly Changing World," *Inside Higher Ed*, January 31, 2013.

73. Stephen R. Porter and Kevin Reilly, "Competency-Based Education as a Potential Strategy to Increase Learning and Lower Costs," HCM Strategists, LLC, July 2014.

74. Anthony DePalma, "Panel Set to Urge Overhaul of Aid for College Students," *The New York Times*, February 3, 1993.

6. UNLEASHING PRIVATE SECTOR INNOVATION

75. Anne Ryman, "Starbucks Workers Start Free Online Classes at ASU," *The Arizona Republic*, October 7, 2014.

76. Ángel González, "Starbucks Will Pay Tuition for Employees to Finish College," *The Seattle Times*, June 17, 2014.

77. "2013 New York Public Library Annual Report," New York Public Library, March, 2014.

78. Douglas Quenqua, "Back to School, Not on a Campus but in a Beloved Museum," January 15, 2012.

79. Robin Pogrebin, "American Museum of Natural History Plans an Addition," *The New York Times*, December 10, 2014.

80. Maya Rhodan, "Obama to Sign Bill Improving Worker Training," *Time*, July 22, 2014.

81. Paul Fain, "Profit and Social Responsibility," *Inside Higher Ed*, August 25, 2014.

82. "World Changing Ideas: A Q & A with Andrew Kassoy, Co-Founder of B Lab," Fastcompany.com, March 4, 2014.

83. Ryan Honeyman, "Has the B Corp Movement Made a Difference?" *Stanford Social Innovation Review*, October 13, 2014.

84. Matthew Tully, "In Rep. Todd Young, a Thoughtful Voice," *Indianapolis Star*, January 24, 2014.

85. John Hartley, "Social Impact Bonds Are Going Mainstream," *Forbes*, September 15, 2014.

7. US DEPARTMENT OF TALENT

86. "Head Start for All," *The Wall Street Journal*, February 27, 2013.

87. Sarah Garland, "A For-Profit Approach to Head Start," *The Hechinger Report*, May 23, 2011.

88. Sarah Garland, "A For-Profit Approach to Head Start," *The Hechinger Report*, May 23, 2011.

89. "One-Stop Career Centers," United States Department of Labor, accessed April 24, 2015.

90. Louis S. Jacobson, "Strengthening One-Stop Career Centers: Helping More Unemployed Workers Find Jobs and Build Skills," Brookings Institution, April 2009.

91. Louis S. Jacobson, "Strengthening One-Stop Career Centers: Helping More Unemployed Workers

Find Jobs and Build Skills," Brookings Institution, April 2009.

92. "Rethinking Pell Grants," College Board Advocacy & Policy Center, April 2013.

93. Statement of Robert B. Reich, Secretary of Labor, Before the Committee on Economics and Educational Opportunities, July 25, 1995.

94. Robert Reich, *The Work of Nations*, Vintage, 1992.

95. "What You Need to Know About the Pell Grant Program," CBS News, September 22, 2014.

96. Daniel B. Wood, "Obama v. Romney 101: 5 Ways They Differ on Immigration," *The Christian Science Monitor*, September 7, 2012.

97. Mitch Daniels Keynote Speech to the Conservative Political Action Committee, February 11, 2011.

8. IMMIGRATION, INNOVATION, INSPIRATION

98. Phillip Ager and Markus Brückner, *Cultural Diversity and Economic Growth: Evidence From the US during the Age of Mass Migration*, 2010.

99. Gianmarco I.P. Ottaviano and Giovanni Peri, "The Economic Value of Cultural Diversity: Evidence from US Cities," *Journal of Economic Geography*, Vol. 6, No. 1, January 2006.

100. Chad Sparber, "Racial Diversity and Macroeconomic Productivity Across US States and Cities," *Regional Studies*, Vol. 44, No. 1, February 2010.

101. Cedric Herring, "Does Diversity Pay?: Race, Gender, and the Business Case for Diversity," *American Sociological Review*, Vol. 74, No. 2, April 2009.

102. Cedric Herring, "Does Diversity Pay?: Race, Gender, and the Business Case for Diversity," *American Sociological Review*, Vol. 74, No. 2, April 2009.

103. Deloitte, Inc., "Only Skin Deep? Re-examining the Business Case for Diversity," September 2011.

104. Christian R. Ostergaard, Bram Timmermans, and Kari Kristinsson, "Does a Different View Create Something New? The Effect of Employee Diversity on Innovation," *Research Policy*, Vol. 40, No. 3, April 2011.

105. Pierpaolo Parrotta, Dario Pozzoli, and Mariola Pytlikova, "The Nexus Between Labor Diversity and Firm's Innovation," *Journal of Population Economics*, Vol. 27, No. 2, April 2014.

106. Orlando C. Richard, "Racial Diversity, Business Strategy, and Firm Performance: A Resource-Based View," *Academy of Management Journal*, Vol. 43, No. 2, April 2000.

107. Orlando C. Richard, B.P. Murthi, and Kiran Ismail, "The Impact of Racial Diversity on Intermediate and Long-Term Performance: The Moderating Role of Environmental Context," *Strategic Management Journal*, Vol. 28, No. 12, December 2007.

108. Lu Hong and Scott E. Page, "Groups of Diverse Problem Solvers Can Outperform Groups of

High-Ability Problem Solvers," *Proceedings of the National Academy of Sciences*, Vol. 101, No. 46, November 16, 2004.

109. Deloitte, Inc., "Only Skin Deep? Re-examining the Business Case for Diversity," September 2011.

110. Eduardo Porter, "Immigration and American Jobs," *The New York Times*, October 19, 2012.

111. Charles Kenney, "To Remain Tops in Innovation, the U.S. Needs Immigration Reform," *BusinessWeek*, July 22, 2013.

112. Vivek Wadhwa, *The Immigrant Exodus: Why America Is Losing the Global Race to Capture Entrepreneurial Talent*, Wharton Digital Press, 2012.

113. Australian Government Department of Immigration and Citizenship, Introduction of New Points Test, November 2010.

114. Mark Cully, "Skilled Migration Selection Policies: Recent Australian Reforms," Australian Government Department of Immigration and Border Protection, 2012.

115. Peter McDonald, "Australia's Ageing Population Poses Risks for Budgets," Australian National University, July 2014.

116. Australian Government Department of Immigration and Border Protection, Migration Programme Statistics, updated February 13, 2015.

117. Mark Cully, "How Much Do Migrants Account for the Unexpected Rise for the Labour Force Participation Rate in Australia over the Past

Decade?" Australian Conference of Economists, 2011.

118. Mark Cully, "How Much Do Migrants Account for the Unexpected Rise for the Labour Force Participation Rate in Australia over the Past Decade?" Australian Conference of Economists, 2011.

119. Tamar Jacoby, "Selecting for Integration? What Role for a Point System?" the German Marshall Fund, December 15, 2010.

120. Joann Muller, "Welcome to Cummins U.S.A.," *Forbes*, April 16, 2014.

9. RESTORING THE RAPIDS—CITIES AS TALENT HUBS

121. Bankrupt Cities, Municipalities List and Map, *Governing Magazine*, updated November 7, 2014.

122. Richard Florida, "America's Best Places for a Raise Since the Great Recession," CityLab from *The Atlantic*, September 17, 2012.

123. "Thousands Create 'American Pie' YouTube Video to Prove Grand Rapids Is Not a Dying City," MiNBC News, May 27, 2011.

124. Jeffery Kaczmarczyk, "Roger Ebert Calls Rob Bliss' Grand Rapids Lip Dub Video the Greatest Music Video Ever Made," Michigan Live, May 30, 2011.

125. Gordon Olson, "A Short History of Grand Rapids, Michigan," City of Grand Rapids.

126. "History," Van Andel Arena, accessed April 24, 2015.

127. Monica Scott, "Grand Rapids Schools Make Strides in Improving Graduation Rates," Michigan Live, March 6, 2014.

128. "Engine Making City in Southern Indiana Boasts a Diesel-Powered Partnership," Lumina Foundation Focus, Summer 2014.

129. "Engine Making City in Southern Indiana Boasts a Diesel-Powered Partnership," Lumina Foundation Focus, Summer 2014.

10. THE SECOND AMERICAN CENTURY

130. Alexander Burns, "Politico Poll: Alarm, Anxiety as Election Looms," Politico, October 20, 2014.

131. Anthony P. Carnevale and Stephen J. Rose, "The Undereducated American," Georgetown University Center on Education and the Workforce, June 26, 2011.

132. Anthony P. Carnevale, Stephen J. Rose, Ben Cheah, "The College Payoff," Georgetown University Center on Education and the Workforce, August 5, 2011.

133. Susan Cantrell and David Smith, *Workforce of One: Revolutionizing Talent Management Through Customization*, Harvard Business Review Press, 2010.

134. Anthony P. Carnevale, Andrew R. Hanson, and Artem Gulish, "Failure to Launch: Structural Shift and the New Lost Generation," Georgetown University Center on Education and the Workforce, September 2013.

135. Anthony P. Carnevale and Stephen J. Rose, "The Undereducated American," Georgetown University Center on Education and the Workforce, June 26, 2011.

136. Malgorzata Kuczera and Simon Field, "A Skills Beyond School Review of the United States," OECD Reviews of Vocational Education and Training, July 10, 2013.

137. Richard Desjardins and Arne Jonas Warnke, "Ageing and Skills: A Review and Analysis of Skill Gain and Skill Loss Over the Lifespan and Over Time," OECD Education Working Papers No. 72, March 27, 2012.

138. "OECD Skills Outlook 2013: First Results from the Survey of Adult Skills," Organization for Economic Cooperation and Development, November 2013.

139. David H. Autor, "Skills, Education, and the Rise of Earnings Inequality Among the 'Other 99 percent,'" *Science*, Vol. 344, No. 6186, May 2014.

140. J. Bradford Delong, "How Fast Is Modern Economic Growth?" Economic Letter, Federal Reserve Bank of San Francisco, October 16, 1998.

141. Randall Lane, "Here's a Plan to Turn Around U.S. Education—and Generate $225 Trillion," *Forbes*, December 1, 2014.

142. Michael Christian, "Human Capital Accounting in the United States: Context, Measurement, and Application," Wisconsin Center for Education Research, Bureau of Economic Analysis, July 2011.

CONCLUSION

143. "America's Got Talent, 2016 Edition," Bloomberg, October 7, 2014.

144. Susan Page, "This Year Was Bad: Next Year? Maybe Worse," *USA Today*, December 11, 2014.

INDEX